How to Win
the Woman
of Your Dreams

By Eric Weber

HOW TO PICK UP GIRLS
HOW TO WIN BACK THE ONE YOU LOVE
SEPARATE VACATIONS (FICTION)

How to Win
the Woman
of Your Dreams

ERIC WEBER

DOUBLEDAY & COMPANY, INC.
GARDEN CITY, NEW YORK
1984

ISBN 0-385-18847-1
Library of Congress Catalog Card Number: 82–46051
Printed in the United States of America
First edition

Library of Congress Cataloging in Publication Data

Weber, Eric, 1942–
   How to win the woman of your dreams.

   1. Dating (Social customs)   2. Women—Psychology.
3. Interpersonal relations.   I. Title.
HQ801.W593   1984   646.7′7

Contents

Introduction

Twelve years ago, when I wrote the book *How to Pick Up Girls,* I did not have lofty expectations. My aim was simply to produce a concise and helpful book on a subject that gives a lot of men a lot of trouble. I knew the book would have an audience. But I was totally unprepared for its overall impact.

To date, *How to Pick Up Girls* has sold two million copies, and sales are still going strong. It has also been translated into six languages, spawned companion books, brought about counterpart books for women, and been made into a television movie. But I knew that the book had really come of age when Johnny Carson started making it the butt of jokes on "The Tonight Show." *How to Pick Up Girls* had made its mark on the American scene.

To the same degree that I was unprepared for the impact that the book would have on the public, I was unprepared for the impact that the success of the book would have on me. Suddenly I was thrust into the limelight. I became a recognized authority on a subject that was getting more and more attention—male-female relationships. Questions and anecdotes came my way by the hundred. Recently many of the questions have had a startlingly similar theme: How do you develop a relationship with a woman *after* you pick her up? How do you ask her out for a date, and then a second and a third and an eighteenth? How do you establish genuine feelings of warmth and affection? How do you get her to like you? How do you take her to bed? Sometimes, even, how do you get her to marry you?

I decided it was time for a sequel. And just as I did when I wrote *How to Pick Up Girls,* I went straight to the source. I began interviewing women, scores of them, to find out what they're looking for from a man today.

Only this time I interviewed slightly older women, ones in their mid-twenties on up, instead of the eighteen- to twenty-two-year-olds I talked to for *How to Pick Up Girls.* It seems to me my readers have grown older and more sophisticated over the past decade. The guy who used *How to Pick Up Girls* back in high school is in his late twenties, living away from home, probably in a big city somewhere. Perhaps he has been to college, maybe even to graduate school, and has landed himself a job. He's a guy who's been around a bit, maybe even married and divorced already. The women he interacts with now are just that—women, no longer girls—and may have careers every bit as important to them as his is to him. They may be better-educated and as witty, as clever, as glib, and certainly as used to the give-and-take, the con and hype, the push and pull of modern-day life among the singles.

What I asked of all these intelligent, independent women is this: "How can a man get involved with you? What are the things you expect from him in a deep, lasting relationship?"

Their answers form the heart (maybe *brain* is a better

word) of this book. For what I learned from today's women is so mind-opening and gives a man so much cause for hope that nothing I could have told you without their input would have been one tenth as helpful, one tenth as insightful.

If there is a central theme to *How to Win the Woman of Your Dreams,* it is that forming relationships with women—with beautiful, interesting, charming, one-hundred-percent desirable women—is not that hard to do. Oh, sure, there are a few prerequisites. You have to be able to walk, to talk, to take a shower. If you can, you've already got the key in the ignition, and now all I'm going to do, with the help of the women I interviewed, is to show you how to start the car and drive it—an operation that you'll find a great deal simpler than you probably imagined.

Another aim of this book is to dispel myths that hinder men as they try to form relationships with women. Here's the first one: Many men believe that there is something magical or mystical about relating to the opposite sex. There isn't. Believe me, crystal balls would only get in the way. Furthermore, there is no "Dating Game" host in the sky who's in control of who finds the woman of his dreams. The simple, stark, powerful truth of the matter is that *you determine it,* using only your personality and other resources.

Now, I'm not denying that every once in a while a relationship does develop right out of the blue, the way it would in the movies—an adventurous hero type meets a beautiful, virginal, modern-day princess type, and they fall instantly and absolutely in love. I mean, I suppose that happens occasionally, that phenomenon which has gotten more publicity than any other human occurrence—*love at first sight.* Who's to say that it absolutely can't? But what I do know is that it has never happened to me, it has never happened to anyone I know, and chances are that it will never happen to you. So I want you to stop waiting for it, if that's what you've been doing.

I also want you to break out of the bad mental habit that a lot of men fall into as kids and never fully grow out of—cursing their fate that they weren't born James Bond or some equally perfect all-around stud. James Bond and his ilk exist in only one place—on celluloid.

Instead of either moping and hoping for the "right" woman to enter your life, or wailing and flailing at the stars for casting you as "Joe Average," it's time to take practical steps toward ensuring that you do have more sustained and satisfying contact with the fairer sex. This book is crammed with strategies, approaches, procedures, and techniques that will guarantee you success. These are not the abstract, vague, "find yourself" type notions that litter most self-help books; these are clear, precise, and concrete, the kind of tips I'd bet you ten bucks would work if you and I made a bet while in a bar.

You may not follow every suggestion you come across in this book, but even if you were inclined to try out only about twenty percent of them, you'd still have enough material to keep you busy for years. I know that because these suggestions are time-tested and foolproof; they've evolved from years of experience and scores of interviews. So smile; there's going to be a lot of action coming your way.

Now, what the contact that this book inspires you to have with women ultimately leads to is up to you. It may mean marriage, or it may mean a lot of one-night stands. Both can be pleasant. But my first piece of advice is not to worry about long-term consequences. For the time being, just get into the ballpark and play the game.

You might ask why I call it a "game"? I choose that metaphor because it gets at the root of my philosophy of both love and life—neither should be taken *too seriously*. In both of them you should try to relax, get loose, and have a lot of fun. Almost paradoxically, it's when you start to have fun at something that you meet with the greatest success.

Now the notion of calling male-female relationships a

"game" is very unpopular these days. People act as if they're above that sort of thing. But that comes from having a victim complex, from thinking that somebody always has to lose when games are played—and that most of the time, it's going to be them. I don't buy that whole line of reasoning. The kind of game I have in mind is more like hide-and-seek than it is like football: more happy, carefree, boundless—and bruiseless.

Of course, you can get bruised if you set yourself up for it psychologically. But we'll be going over all the hidden pitfalls to help you avoid them.

At the same time, *How to Win the Woman of Your Dreams* is not about beating women in some way. I believe that the guy who gets beyond the "war of the sexes" morality is the guy who will inspire women to get beyond it, too. And that means a better time for the both of them.

Sure, some of this book is about being "manipulative"—but not in the mean, petty sense of the word. As you'll see, it's about giving in to pressure as well as exerting it, letting the force of natural human attraction just take over. So in order to make the advice I give here truly effective, you're going to have to pick up to some degree on the spirit of it, as well as the mechanics. What this basically will entail is a letting go of the attitude that "I am not going to make an ass out of myself, I am not going to be stupid." What those words really mean is that you're unwilling to take any chances; and that makes you like an empty glass, hoping that somebody will come along to fill you up.

There is no need to wait. This book will show you how to make it happen.

How to Win
the Woman
of Your Dreams

1

The All-Natural Approach

A few chapters from now we're going to discuss a subject that seems to be of paramount interest to every talk-show host, disc jockey, and reporter who has ever interviewed me —opening lines.

For the present, however, I'd like to explore three areas that I am convinced are far more fundamental to breaking the ice with an appealing stranger than your initial set of words. And by those I mean attitude, style, and presentation.

What's the use of borrowing a witty opening line from Woody Allen if, although you're a nice guy, you're not all that funny? And why bother to come on suave and urbane if the real you is a country boy, relaxed, laid-back, ingenuous?

No, the magic of an opening line is hardly magical if it misrepresents you or promises something different from what you are ultimately going to deliver. Rather, it should be consistent with the real you, a natural outgrowth of what you *feel* like saying, of what you are capable of saying—in short, not a "line" at all. And that leads me to the following point: The *best* way to introduce yourself to a new woman is to be natural, to be yourself.

If you have any doubts about that, I urge you to spend some time observing salesmen or anyone else to whom the act of starting a conversation with strangers has become routine, a commonplace part of everyday life.

What happens when it's your job to be constantly introducing yourself to strangers is that the ritual soon loses its ability to terrify you. You stop devising clever opening gambits and instead gain confidence in what comes naturally to mind. Your fear of rejection diminishes—partly because you discover rejection isn't nearly as damaging as you thought it would be, and partly because you see that far fewer people are rejecting you than you anticipated. At the same time your confidence in your basic personality mushrooms. You find that, by and large, people are pretty much the same all over and don't expect you, nor even *want* you, to be endlessly witty and clever and glib. The ordinary relaxed conversation that is the backbone of your relationships with friends works just as well with strangers.

Picture, for example, how a traveling salesman might address a cocktail waitress at the bar of the motel where he's put up for the night. He doesn't sit there for an hour, intense and preoccupied, as he plots an opening gambit to spring on her. Rather, he's much more likely to say, "Oh, boy, what a day."

The waitress is apt to respond, "Tough day, huh?"

"You're not kidding. I've been on the road since six o'clock. How about you?"

"Oh, not too bad. I didn't go on until about an hour ago."

"Are you new here? I don't remember you from last September when I passed through."

"No, I worked a different shift then. Afternoons."

And so on and so on. Not exactly Shakespeare, perhaps, but sufficient to start a conversation rolling.

Now let's analyze what happened here. The salesman didn't ask a question, didn't make an overture, didn't want to know the waitress' sign, didn't tell her she had great legs. He just gave vent to a natural *feeling* he was having—he'd had a tough day. And because the waitress didn't feel on the spot, propositioned, pursued, or hit upon in any way, she felt free to respond in kind, naturally falling into conversation with the man as if they'd known each other for years. In short the waitress was gently drawn into the salesman's life because he was making no demands, creating no tension. She could pick up on or ignore his harmless remark, as she saw fit.

The critical question, of course, is "Can *you* do the same?" Can you learn to be the same easygoing, comfortable person around strangers that you are around friends?

I heartily urge you to give it a try. It's simply a matter of shaking up your mind-set. For example, let's imagine that you're at a party, sitting near a woman you haven't met yet but would sorely like to. Instead of tensing your jaw muscles and staring at her out of the corner of your eye as you feverishly try to create a line that will blow her away, think to yourself that you know her already, that she's an old friend, one who rather likes you, in fact. Lean back, put your hands behind your head, gaze about the room in amusement, and declare, "I've never seen so many striped ties in one place in my life." Or, "Yuck! That's the worst dip I've ever tasted." Or voice aloud any other observation you'd be likely to make if the person sitting nearby really were a close buddy rather than a stranger. In other words, say something you'd be apt to say simply because it occurred to you and needed venting rather than something designed to make a girl interested in you.

I can't guarantee that the woman you have your eye on will immediately leap into your lap and say you're her kind of guy. I can't even promise that she'll respond at all. But even if she doesn't, there's absolutely no reason to feel rejected. After all, you just tossed a comment into the air, not aimed at anyone in particular, and were only half expecting an answer.

But then experience indicates that more than one out of two times you will get an answer. Casual, low-key remarks tossed offhandedly into the air are the easiest kind to pick up on. They invite the listener in because they make no demands upon her, require no commitment. They demonstrate that you're not a pickup artist, hysterically on the make, but rather a friendly, easygoing guy who likes his fellow man and woman and isn't necessarily out to bed everyone in sight.

Okay, you've tossed out your casual remark, the same kind of observation you might have made to your best friend Mike. This isn't Mike sitting next to you, though, but rather a marvelously good-looking redheaded woman in a pale pink sweater and black velvet slacks. Her perfume gently suffuses the air about you, drawing you toward her, intensifying your attraction. But you haven't come on strong; you've kept things light, merely remarking that it's a great night for a party. What happens next?

Let's make it tough on you. Red doesn't respond. It's as if you're not there or you haven't said anything at all. Do you panic? Do you revert back to old ways, get serious all of a sudden, clear your throat to hide your nervousness, and declare in a formal voice, "I've been yearning to meet you all night long"?

No. Stay loose. You may want to aim your next comment at her a little more directly, but keep it light and natural. Try to maintain the mind-set that you *know* her, not that she's a stranger you're trying to know. For example . . .

YOU: So how was your day?
SHE: Huh?

YOU: I said, how was your day? Busy?

SHE: Not really.

YOU: God, mine sure was. The market went crazy today. You have any stocks?

SHE: I think I have five shares of AT&T my grandfather gave me for graduation.

YOU: Hey, you're in luck. You made fifteen bucks today.

SHE: I did?

YOU: Yep. AT&T went up three points. This is some night for a party, isn't it?

SHE: I guess.

YOU: I mean the weather today. It's so crisp and cool out there. I love the fall.

SHE: I know what you mean. It's nice when all that awful humidity is over with.

YOU: Yeah, it makes you feel energetic. And hungry. Did you try the hors d'oeuvres?

SHE: No. Any good?

YOU: Not bad. I'll bring back a plateful.

And there you have it—a full-scale, friendly, loose-as-a-goose conversation, started *casually*, without risk, without an *obvious* goal.

Remember, friendliness begets friendliness, casualness casualness. If your previous attempts to strike up conversations with women have been marked by tension and plotting—the sort of grim determination I often see on men's faces who are about to pounce on a woman—try to lighten up. Pretend you're going over to say hello to someone who really likes you, someone you've known for years. "Can you believe all this rain we're having!" is a lot more likely to put a woman at ease than "You have a lovely figure."

I'm not saying the latter can't work. But why not wait until you've gotten to know one another a little better, when your easygoing friendliness has put her into a relaxed, receptive mood. For starters it's generally better to stick to noncontroversial, impersonal remarks. That way you're much more likely to get a conversation really rolling.

Where and how else can you use this simple low-key approach to meeting new women? Almost anywhere. In church, for example, during the minister's sermon you can casually whisper to no one in particular, "He's good today, isn't he? Full of fire and brimstone." But, again, only if *that* is what you are feeling. If you're bored out of your mind, give vent to that instead.

At the beach you might try, "Better not go out too far. The undertow is murder."

If you've managed to hail the hot-dog vendor at the ballpark, why not turn to a nearby woman and inquire if she too wants a frank? You can even treat her if you want: "Don't be silly. This one's on me. You can get dessert when the Cracker Jack kid comes around."

Meeting women becomes tension-filled when you yourself are tense, when you feel there's a lot at stake. Put scoring out of your mind. You are simply chatting for a few minutes with a fellow human being. If something develops, fine. And if nothing much comes of it, that's also fine.

There are tens of millions of other women out there. The more of them you meet, the more likely you are to get something going with one. Keep it light. According to a healthy majority of the women I queried on the subject, that's the way they prefer it.

"I like it when a man talks to me about light things at first," says a ski instructor from Colorado. "It's so much easier to deal with."

Wendy, an actress from San Francisco, agrees. "I'll talk to almost anyone, as long as they're not trying to find out my life story. Men make the mistake of thinking they can somehow *make* you fall in love with them on sight. They come on so somber so much of the time, so serious, as if they're getting ready to propose. I have to let a man's vibrations flow around me for ten or fifteen minutes before I can tell if anything's there. And I don't like to be under any pressure while I'm doing it. The best thing is just a light, almost offhand conversation. If nothing clicks, well, then nobody gets hurt."

To summarize, the world's best pickup technique is to act as nonchalant and relaxed with strangers as you do among friends. If you can manage that, you can meet just about any woman you want . . . naturally.

2

Meet Markets

One of the first myths I want to lay to rest about where to meet women is that singles bars are the best. They're the best all right, but only if you have the smoky good looks of Richard Gere, or Bill Murray's gift of insane humor, or the fast-talking brassiness of Richard Dreyfuss. But the average guy's looks, humor, and brassiness are less than great—so much less than great, in fact, that I think of them as sort of a national disaster.

The problem, of course, is that singles bars *look* so damn good—so glittery, so tempting, so full of possibilities. You bop down First Avenue on Manhattan's East Side or Sunset Boulevard in Beverly Hills and all of a sudden there's this great thump of rock and roll wafting through the night, quickening your pulse, calling you in. And then when you *do* stick your head in, there're all those long blond manes bouncing to the beat of the giant overhead speakers, all those tight be-Sasson-ed behinds shimmying, and you think to yourself, *My God, a man could get laid in there.*

Unfortunately, far fewer men get laid on the singles-bar circuit than one would imagine. That's because most of the girls you'll run across in a singles bar on any particular night seem to have a certain bizarre mind-set. It goes kind of like this: *Look, I doubt that any guy I meet here is going to respect me enough to call me again, so I might as well really cut loose and do something scandalous, shoot for someone over my head, have a zipless fuck with John Travolta's twin.*

Women in singles bars are looking to get laid, but unfortunately rarely with the dependable, responsible, unglamorous kind of guy they're likely to marry. No, tonight they want a superstar, someone tall, charismatic, lean, hard, and dashing.

Now, all this doesn't mean that the female habitués of singles bars can't be had by someone *less* dashing than the hunk of their fantasies. They most certainly can. But more often than not it takes a guy with a hell of a lot of balls, perseverance, and bravura to do it. And judging from the guys I've met over the years, I've come to the conclusion that most of us, save for theatrical agents and clothes salesmen, just don't have the fast-talking delivery and leathery exterior that make a man immune to the slings and arrows of the singles-bar wars.

So I ask this: Why expose yourself needlessly to an environment that holds so little promise when there are so many better, friendlier, richer arenas in which to meet terrific women? Forget the long blond manes, if you can. Forget the quadraphonic jukeboxes. Forget the glitter and the bouncing bosoms and the highly charged, insinuating atmosphere. There is far less there than meets the eye, particularly for those of us mortals who are possessed of the normal amount of shyness, sensitivity, and self-doubt. Superman, Captain Marvel, Clint Eastwood—these are the fearless macho males we are all supposed to be like. But in reality most of us are much more fragile. And so I say to hell with singles bars. Let's explore terrain on which a man is far more likely to meet a woman who will like him back. There are dozens of fertile meeting places nearly every which way we turn. And they are so much more rewarding than singles bars that it's not even a contest.

For example, have you ever thought about taking singing lessons? *Singing lessons!? What, is this man mad? I have the voice of a bullfrog, Tiny Tim's sense of pitch. And what does singing have to do with girls?*

Plenty. Although millions of people *like* to sing, women are more apt to come out of the shower about it. Check out your school chorus or church choir. If the women don't outnumber the men at least two to one, I've been seeing double.

A young actress who does role-playing in my "How to Meet Women" course in New York City mentioned that she took group singing lessons in an attempt to meet men. The class consisted of thirty-three women and five men. She says she'll be lucky to get an ankle.

Hmm, you may be musing, *that's almost seven women for every man. That's not bad.* And, indeed, it isn't. But what are you going to do about it? It is one thing to feel a surge of excitement, an impulse to take action, while reading a book to help you fall asleep at night. It is another thing to get up the next morning, haul out the old seven-pound phone book, and begin tracking down choirs, choruses, music schools, and adult night courses in singing. It takes a bit of searching, of asking around. We all know how much easier it is to relax and fall back into doing nothing, to heed the narcotic call of our local singles bar, and to blow yet another Friday night and twenty-five dollars on stingers.

Well, resist the singles-bar call. Stop being a singles-bar junkie. And get out the phone directory. Because if you really want to change your life . . . *you* have to change your life. And that means doing something different . . . enduring the little bit of hard work it takes to track down the right singing course, living through the mild embarrassment of having your friends or folks find out about your new endeavor.

But picture this: You walk into a class of thirty-three attractive, pleasant, responsive-looking women, all turning to check you out as you take your place among them. Imagine the relaxed, friendly atmosphere. Luxuriate in the easy, casual manner with which the pretty dark-eyed woman sitting next to you says, "How was your day?" or simply, "My name is Karen." That's got to be better than walking into a dark den of standoffish women who have made up their minds ahead of time that they don't want to have anything to do with any man short of Warren Beatty.

What other promising places are there to meet women? A friend of mine took a yoga class at a new–life-style kind of school in suburban New Jersey. The particular night he went, there were eight women and three men in attendance —not the same staggering odds as in the singing course but odds stacked in a man's favor nonetheless. The women, by and large, were young, appealing, and, as one might expect in a yoga class, in wonderful shape. The students spent two hours twisting and turning on their woven mats. Afterward they retired to a coed sauna room where my friend was stunned, and not in the least displeased, to discover that several of the women were steaming themselves topless.

The next week he signed up for a full semester of massage courses. These were attended most nights by nine women and two men. What one does in a massage course is knead and caress his classmates. You can imagine how much more conducive this is to starting a relationship than walking up to a total stranger in a crowded bar and asking, "Didn't you go to Ohio State?" Why, I venture to say the very same woman who would answer, "No, you creep, I never been outta Brooklyn," when approached in a saloon, might purr luxuriantly under your touch in massage class. Which, in case you haven't divined it yet, is one of the main points of this chapter: THE SAME WOMAN WHO MIGHT BE

COLD TO YOU IN A SINGLES BAR MIGHT BE DELIGHTED TO
MEET YOU IN A DIFFERENT ENVIRONMENT.

So why knock your head against the wall? Seek out
women in different environments. One of my students reports that he is taking a dance exercise class. He says he is
the only male in the class and that many of his classmates
are delighted to have finally come across someone of the
opposite sex who shares their passion for dance (more
about this later). There are two other benefits, explains
Maurice. The women exercise in deliciously scant Dan-
skins, and several of them actually seem to be competing
for his attention. I am not surprised. Put one rooster, no
matter how scrawny, among one hundred hens, and that
poor bantam will be needing vitamin B_1 shots within the
week.

Where else do women outnumber men in a nurturing,
nonthreatening atmosphere? Supermarkets, that's where.
Next time you need to pick up a six-pack, stop in at your
local Kroger's/Grand Union/IGA and check out the meat
counter. Pick up a leg of lamb and study it as if there is
something profoundly confusing about it. Ask the next attractive woman who passes if you fry these babies up like a
hot dog. You don't, of course, and she'll be horrified at the
prospect of your ruining twenty-seven dollars' worth of
perfectly fine food. Watch how eager and pleased she is to
be the expert, to come to your rescue, emotional and perhaps otherwise. If it feels right, try to engage her in conversation that goes beyond the carnivorous. Under circumstances like this, it is often quite easy. What could be
threatening to a woman about talking cooking with a nice
man in a supermarket?

Flatter her. Tell her you bet she's a terrific cook. Find out
if she lives in the neighborhood. Ask for her phone number; if she seems a touch leery, then request her number
where she works. Tell her you'd simply like to repay her
kindness by taking her out to lunch (more about this later,

as well). To many women, lunch is a first date that's far less of a commitment than a weekend at your cabin in the woods. Don't be surprised if this budding new relationship leads to an invitation to dinner—and a whole lot sooner than you think.

What do you do if you have no real need to stop in at a supermarket? Go anyway, even if only to buy a pack of gum. What if the first woman you talk to has a wedding band on? So what? You're simply asking her advice on matters culinary; not to perform cunnilingus on her.

I am constantly amazed at the fears and complications raised by many of the men who seek out my advice. *But, Eric, what if there's no supermarket on my block? What if the A&P is out of leg of lamb that day?* Well, then improvise, for God's sake. Be creative. Stop in at a butcher store instead. Ask her how long it takes to boil a pork chop. If she's married, enjoy the little exchange for what it's worth. And if you feel gutsy enough, tell her that if she ever, God forbid, gets separated, you'd like to be the first one to know. Then give her your card and wait for another pretty woman to happen by.

But whatever you do, don't let the "what ifs" defeat you. Certainly life can suddenly become complicated and unpredictable. But what if you sit glued to your stool at your neighborhood pub trying to solve all the "what ifs" ahead of time? Why, you'll never take action. And that would be a shame. Because I can assure you that no matter how unexpected the developments you encounter in a supermarket, they are still bound to yield many more dates, hugs, and kisses than those that turn up in a singles bar.

Another fine and out-of-the-ordinary place to meet women is in a cooking course. These are offered just about everywhere—in night classes at local high schools and colleges, at most adult education centers, and, of course, at cooking schools themselves. A course in which you participate—that is, actually do the cooking yourself—is better than a pure demonstration. Obviously it is much easier to fall into conversation with a fellow classmate when both you and she can share an experience—she scalds her hand on a saucepan, for example, and you have an extra slab of butter with which to anoint her. Once again, in order to take a cooking course you have to get off your butt and sign up, no matter how tiresome a chore it is, no matter how silly you feel. But remember, it is those men who have the daring and energy to do the unusual who do best with women.

One of my students mentioned that he took a Chinese-cooking course. He and the other people in the class, nine women and one lone hombre, all stood around a long counter chopping vegetables and adding spices. After sampling one another's *woo hip har* all night long, he said he felt entirely natural asking the woman working to his left out for coffee. She readily agreed. Today they are dating.

One of the best ways to meet women—far, far from the madding crowds of singles bars and discos—is to get involved in some kind of group activity related to a hobby or interest of yours. That way, even if nothing romantic pans out, you won't be wasting your time. Are you a movie buff? Take a film-appreciation course. My experience is that such courses are peopled largely by women. Often a well-known director or scriptwriter will appear as a guest lecturer; so at least you'll have an enjoyable, fascinating night at the flicks, even if there isn't a single woman present who appeals to you. But then, that's not what I would expect; the women I meet who are interested in film are, for some reason, unusually good-looking. And once again, the environment of a small, cozy theater full of intelligent, simpatico people has to be a more convivial place than a noisy bar jammed with folks hysterically on the make.

How do you find a film-appreciation course? In Chicago, New York, Boston, Los Angeles, San Francisco, Houston, or any other big city, it's easy. Often such courses are run by a major art museum or university. Or scour the newspaper for lectures on film or special screenings. You'll find that once you put yourself on the alert for a particular type of event it starts popping up all over.

Are you into exercise or swimming? Join a coed health club. An attractive typist I know, who has just joined the rapidly expanding ranks of female weight lifters, tells me the Nautilus room at her health club is coed and thus "sexy as hell." Sounds that way to me, too, what with all those luscious, curvy girls in their leotards straining to develop their pecs.

If you like taking pictures, join a photography club. Or if you've always wanted to paint or act, for God's sake, take painting or acting lessons. They're an unbelievable amount of fun and an almost automatic way to meet hip, modern women.

I can't guarantee you, of course, that any of the above would yield the dividend of a beautiful new person to date. But look at it this way. Anything *new* you experience is broadening and makes a fuller, more interesting person of you. And I can guarantee you that "interesting" is one of the traits women look for most in a man.

A great way to combine decorating your apartment or home inexpensively with meeting lots of new women is to visit a flea market. Held on weekends, these vast shopping grounds are usually teeming with attractive ladies—some customers, others manning (or should I say "womaning") their own booths. I can't think of an easier way to meet a woman than to walk up to the booth in which she markets quilts to check one out for your bed.

But what if I have no interests or hobbies? Well, then invent one. Or just throw fate to the wind and take a group bicycle trip, or sign up for a ski tour, or attend a poetry reading, or take a ceramics class, or do anything else that sounds as if it just might possibly (a) involve women, and (b) be fun. Certainly gambling a few bucks on an activity that at the very least will be mind-opening is better than once again squandering your hard-earned dollars on sudsy beer in a bar, the sole result of which may be to make you feel frustrated, bitter, and not very good about yourself at the end of the evening.

To change your life you literally have to change your life. That means doing something differently from the way you're doing it now. And one way to do that is to extricate yourself from the singles-bar rut and visit new places, places which the world doesn't think of as happy hunting grounds but which in reality are rife with pretty, pleasant, interested women, women who at the drop of a phrase will happily fall into conversation with you. Believe me, they're out there, millions of them. And if you'll just give some of the above suggestions a try, you'll start meeting and dating and hugging and kissing and loving them more easily and quickly than you ever thought possible.

3

Icebreakers
to Warm Her Up

Now that we've just discovered a whole raft of great new
places to meet women, here are a few very good opening
lines to help you break the ice. In addition I've tried to
suggest where, when, and how to use these potent conversation openers. You don't want to lean way over to the
woman sharing your pew at religious services and whisper,
"You have a delicious sexual aroma about you." On second
thought . . .

Of course, if you already are an expert at meeting women
and are just reading this chapter to heighten your skills, you
will probably want to adapt the lines to your own style and
rhythm of speech. But if, like most of us, you are prone to
bouts of nervousness and insecurity when approaching a
strange woman, please feel free to use the lines *verbatim*.
That's what they are there for—to give you a carefully
thought-out formula for success that you can mouth aloud
like a speech in a play. It's tough enough dredging up the

courage to walk up to a girl you don't know without having the additional burden of inventing something clever or winning to say to her. So make it easy on yourself. Use any or all of the following ten opening lines to your heart's content. You'll be stunned and delighted at how instantaneously they can turn a total stranger into a woman who is smiling at you, batting her eyes, cocking her head coquettishly, and eager to hear more of your sweet, endearing voice.

AT A PARTY OR A DANCE. Things are just starting to pick up. The room is crowded, music is blaring, and men and women are beginning to dance. Those who aren't are standing around chatting and looking one another over. Now is the time to select the one woman in the crowd who moves you more than all the rest.

Study her for a bit from afar. You won't actually be speaking to her yet, of course, but just by watching her for a few minutes you'll get a sense of who she is, what she is like. Then, by the time you do approach her, you will feel as if you know her slightly, which should make you a trifle more comfortable in her presence than if you'd just suddenly been plopped down at her side. You will have also developed a sense of whether or not she is here with anyone. You don't want to apply the magic line I'm about to suggest to a woman whose date is a psychotic-looking linebacker.

Okay, now you've spent the prescribed five or ten minutes observing her. You've seen her smile, take two figs off the hors d'oeuvres table, tap her foot with unbridled enthusiasm to a Springsteen song, and stare with more than cursory interest at the Mondrian print on the wall. Detective that you've become, you store all this away in your crafty little mind. Later it may come in handy. Now it is time for you to approach this lovely creature you long to meet.

Walk casually up to her. Smile. Try to keep the crazed look of intensity and anxiety that may be welling up inside you out of your eyes. *You* know you have no plans to strangle this girl. But does she? Men often fail to consider a woman's actual mind-set when approaching her. You may assume she just can't wait to reject you, so you get ready for the worst. The resulting fear and bitterness may show on your face. And this can frighten a woman. You must try to keep in mind that instead of having readied herself to shoot down all suitors but Burt Reynolds, the girl you are approaching is far more likely to be in a pleasant, outgoing mood, eager to meet new people whom she will enjoy. Help nurture her good mood by looking like someone she *will* enjoy, not like the hapless, nervous, sure-you're-going-to-be-spurned chap you feel like inside.

It's easy, of course, for me to tell you to lighten up as I'm sitting here behind my typewriter in my cozy den. But nevertheless, you must try. Relax your face. Smile. You'd be astonished at how deep a vein of insecurity a little grin will hide.

Now what the hell do you say to her? It's simple. The truth. And if you're wondering what that is, allow me to put it in words for you: "I just want you to know that I've been here about fifteen minutes, studying every woman in the place." Pause for a moment and shake your head as if mildly awed. "No one even comes close to you."

Then just stand back and watch the response to your prose. I can't guarantee that she'll immediately sign on as your indentured servant for life, but I am willing to predict that she will suddenly find herself rather predisposed to wanting to spend some time with you. Who among us doesn't like to hear wonderful things about himself? Who doesn't want to hear more? And since you've already done a pretty good job once, the woman you've approached has reason to believe you have other intoxicating compliments up your sleeve. For example, "I see you've got good taste. You like Springsteen. And Mondrian."

Oh, and if you're thinking that maybe "no one else

comes close" is too obvious a come-on, consider the reaction of an attractive young woman in my office. When asked how she'd respond to "no one at this party comes close to you," she replied, "I'd probably think it was bullshit." Then she grinned delightedly. "But I wouldn't care. Because, if a man singled me out to say that, he'd probably think I was the prettiest one there anyway."

ON A COMMUTER BUS OR TRAIN. You walk down the aisle looking for a seat. Several yards ahead there is one. And not only that, it's right next to a smashing redhead or blonde, or brunette or whatever this particular morning has been kind enough to throw in your path. Don't be like most men —so certain that the woman can read your horny thoughts that you pass right on by and take the seat next to the obese napping insurance broker whose head will keep tumbling onto your shoulder the whole trip through. The pretty woman with the empty seat next to her *cannot* read your mind. And even if she could, chances are she'd be flattered. (About eighty percent of all women's sexual fantasies seem to relate to men finding them berserkly attractive.) So take the seat you want. It is your right and, if you're truly devoted to winning the woman of your dreams, your duty.

Just because you've managed to find the courage to sit next to her, however, doesn't mean that you should hit up on her right away. Then she *will* know precisely what you're up to. Instead, open your paper and spend five minutes perusing the sports section. And while you're doing it, try to keep from sneaking nervous, darting glances at your seatmate every twelve seconds. No matter how sly you think you're being, she'll sense it; and you'll probably wind up annoying the hell out of her.

All right. Now that five minutes have passed and you've conducted yourself like a mature gentleman, let your brow fall into your hands. Massage your temples. If you can do it without sounding ridiculous, you might even let out with a soft groan. This done, turn to the woman next to you and ask with as little fanfare as possible if she mightn't have an aspirin in her handbag. How? *Comme ci:* "You wouldn't happen to have an aspirin on you by any chance?"

This is all it will take. There is no need to volunteer why you want the aspirin. Most self-respecting women have a deep well of sympathy for their fellow human beings. And whether she has aspirin with her or not, she is almost certain to inquire why you need one. A hangover is glamorous, providing of course that you have shaved well this morning and don't look like a budding young alcoholic. Having stayed up all night working on your novel is another good explanation. So is tension over an important meeting with a new client. All these things say something good about you. And you will be gratified, almost touched, by how deeply concerned she seems about your welfare.

Naturally your performance will be more convincing if you really do have the trace of a headache. But even if you don't, don't be afraid to use this little piece of manipulation. Later, over a cozy dinner in an intimate restaurant, you can confess that you really didn't have a headache at all. It was only that you wanted to meet her so badly. More than likely, she'll be flattered.

WAITING IN LINE ANYWHERE. This next conversation opener was invented by an old friend. We were standing among a group of about twenty-five people, all waiting for tables in a crowded health-food restaurant in midtown Manhattan. Nearby stood an attractive, thin woman in her late twenties, her nose buried in a book. Nodding toward the woman, my friend looked at me as if to say, "Watch this." Tapping the woman on the shoulder, he said, "You look like a country girl."

Somewhat suspicious, the country girl turned to my friend. "Why do you say that?"

"Because you have that peaches-and-cream complexion.

You don't see that much here in New York City in February."

The girl's face broke into a broad, thoroughly enchanted grin, as if my friend had just caressed her with his hands rather than mere words. Now between you and me, I didn't find her complexion to be much different from any of the other women's I noticed in the restaurant. But it sure developed a pink healthy glow after my friend's remark. He invited her to sit with us at our table, and she accepted with genuine excitement.

So if you live in Akron or Cleveland or Milwaukee or Chicago or any other city that gets cold and bleak and gray in the winter, tell a woman with whom you've been thrown in close contact, like on an elevator or in the lobby of a movie theater, that she looks like a country girl. Rarely have I seen a comment work such magic.

IN A LUNCHEONETTE. It's lunch time. You're sitting at the counter having your usual hamburger and fries when the sexless middle-aged spinster to your left vacates her stool and, miracle of miracles, it is snapped up by a svelte, curvaceous twenty-year-old who is just oozing with sex appeal. This doesn't happen every day, Jim, so don't sit there and let her get away. As subtly as you can, have your waiter bring her a 7Up or a Perrier. Then, when she acknowledges your gift, tip your glass to her and declare, "If this place had a liquor license, I'd have made it a champagne cocktail."

Such a remark is (a) flattering, (b) testimony to your potential generosity, and (c) a more unique way of telling her you're attracted to her than "Hi ya there, good-lookin'!"

She will probably smile, maybe even blush a little, and want to know more about this clever stranger who has just made her feel so good in the middle of a humdrum work-day.

ANYWHERE IN THE WORLD. "Hi. You look nice. My name's Joe." Nearly one hundred percent of the women I interviewed for *How to Pick Up Girls* told me that honesty is the best policy, that the very best way to meet them is simply to come up and introduce yourself. The above line is low-key, complimentary, and, in a subtle but undeniable way, makes it very difficult for a woman not to introduce herself back.

IN A LAUNDROMAT. You've finally got around to stuffing into a washing machine the three weeks' worth of laundry that had been piling up in the corner of your room. The attractive woman in the flannel shirt and the dungarees at the machine next to yours is almost finished folding her mound of maddeningly provocative black satin panties. Quick! Don't let her get away. Say something. For example, point to your jumbo-sized box of Tide and ask, "Do I just use half, or do I dump in the whole damn thing?"

If the woman realizes you're kidding (you are, aren't you?), she'll laugh. And that's to your advantage, because more than seventy-five percent of the women I interviewed for *How to Pick Up Girls* volunteered that they are helplessly attracted to men with a good sense of humor.

If she thinks you're serious, she'll take pity on you and want to help. Either way, you've successfully broken the ice with an attractive stranger. And that's what *How to Win the Woman of Your Dreams* is all about.

TO A WOMAN EATING AN APPLE. Actually the following line is uniquely versatile and can be used just about anytime you see a woman do something with gusto: "You really love life, don't you?"

When she asks how you can tell, you simply explain that you never saw anyone eat an apple, step into a tennis ball, walk through the rain, or ride a bicycle with such an obvious sense of enjoyment.

If you've been right about how deeply she enjoys life, she'll be thrilled at your perceptiveness, impressed by the cleverness of your remark, and flattered by the notion that you've been observing her. And what more could you ask from an opening line than that?

TO AN ATTRACTIVE WOMAN ANYWHERE. Recently a friend was browsing in a department store. He had stopped in front of a display of sweaters when suddenly he sensed someone standing nearby. He looked up, and there on the other side of a stack of colorful crewnecks was a woman of such awesome good looks that my friend could hardly breathe. For an instant their glances locked, instantly sending my friend into a trance. As the woman meandered down her aisle, Doug meandered down his, unable to take his eyes off her. He was embarrassed by his blatant ogling but could not help himself. Finally he blurted out, "Listen, I'm sorry I keep staring at you, but I can't take my eyes off you."

The woman blushed and giggled and stammered that that was the nicest thing anyone had said to her in a long time. Later, over a cup of coffee in the store cafeteria, Doug got her telephone number and her agreement to go to the movies with him on the following Friday night. Using his very words, I'll bet you can do the same.

ON THE STREET. A very beautiful woman friend, Amanda, was once walking down Rodeo Drive in Beverly Hills when suddenly a man shot out of a store and blocked her path. "Hold it! Wait a minute," he said, "wait till I think up something to say."

She was so impressed by his spontaneity and honesty, she did. They are going out to this day.

I relate this story because men often ask what's a good way to approach the countless striking women they are constantly encountering on the street. I can't think of a better way.

ANYWHERE. The following line was told to me by my friend and collaborator on *How to Pick Up Women,* Molly Cochran. She claims that the next four words will make any woman melt: "You are so beautiful."

I agree.

I could go on and on with great opening lines. I'm sure there must be millions, because I alone have heard thousands, invented hundreds, and just given you ten of my favorites. You should note that for the most part they are friendly, nonthreatening, not *too* clever, and generally quite flattering. The two exceptions are those that seek advice. They are included because, when you think about it, the very act of asking someone for help is flattering. It says you *trust* her.

Should you stick to the ten lines above forever and ever? Of course not. They are as effective as any I've ever heard, but what is more important is that you say *something,* almost *anything,* rather than let the opportunity, and thus the woman you have your eye on, slip away.

Remember, even if she wants to, chances are a woman is not going to pick you up. You're going to have to make the first move yourself. So do it. Memorize a few of the lines above; or better yet, invent your own. Then when you spot some wonderful woman you're dying to meet, instead of tensing your throat and remaining silent, give in to the opposite impulse. Let the magical words welling up in your throat take voice and float out through your lips. That's all it takes. You'll see. Once an opening line has actually made it into the air, been spoken aloud, it gets heard, enjoyed, embraced, and treasured far more fervently than you could ever fantasize.

4

Shy Man's Guide to Picking Up Girls

For years I've been telling men there's no better way to add more women to their love life than to meet them extemporaneously. Apparently some guys have been listening, for each week I get at least several letters thanking me for my advice. "I was sitting around a fountain in a park in Colorado," writes one young guy from out West. "Sitting right near me was this absolutely smashing-looking blonde, kind of holding her face up to the sun. Normally I would never have had the balls to talk to her, but I remembered what you said about 'say anything,' so I told myself it was now or never. Crawling up the side of the fountain was a spider. It gave me an idea. I cleared my throat to get the girl's attention, then asked, 'Do you think spiders ever sleep?'

"Granted, it's not exactly a line that would have done Woody Allen proud, but for some reason the girl thought it was funny and started laughing. That got me laughing, too, mostly out of relief that she hadn't got up and walked away.

Anyway, we got to talking, exchanged phone numbers, and a few days later I called her up to go horseback riding. Now we're living together, all because I said one dumb thing. If I hadn't said anything, I doubt that we would have ever met at all. It's amazing."

Actually, to me it isn't the least bit amazing. As I've been saying all along, there are tens of millions of women out there just dying for you to come up and get involved with them, and often it's as easy as saying hello. What does amaze me is that so many men still find it such an impossible task. They know in their hearts that it's possible to pick up girls, and sometimes downright easy. Yet something holds them back. They're afraid they'll get rejected. They're afraid they'll run out of things to say. They're afraid they'll screw things up.

Let me tell you something, you guys who are too shy to pick up girls: WOMEN LIKE SHY MEN. WOMEN DON'T MIND A BUMBLING, STUMBLING APPROACH AT ALL.

Oh, sure, Weber, you're probably thinking. *You're just telling us that to build up our confidence. Then once we get out there and give it a try, girls'll reject us so fast it'll make your head spin.*

Not true. I must have interviewed ten thousand women over the past several years, and one of the points they touch upon most frequently is that coming on too slick is the biggest turnoff this side of bad breath. It makes a woman think a guy is a pickup artist.

On the other hand, say the girls, if a guy is shy, if he blushes, if he stutters a little, it makes a woman feel that she's special, that something about her was so incredibly attractive that this poor, shy guy couldn't help himself. He just had to give it a shot. Women like that, your finding them so special and beautiful that you'll risk your life—or your ego anyway—just for the chance of getting to know them.

Let me describe a piece of role-playing that recently took place in my New York City course "How to Talk to

Women." A quiet, balding man in his late twenties was sitting next to Karen, a sensuous dark-haired actress who helps teach the course. The two were pretending they were strangers who just happened to be riding the same bus to work. The man was instructed to start a conversation. Even though it was obviously a set-up situation, he seemed terribly shy about addressing her. Finally, on his fifth try, he blurted out, "Listen, I'm usually much too nervous to talk to a woman as pretty as you. I can hardly think of anything to say." Then he blushed like crazy.

So did the actress. What the hell was going on here? Karen explained that the man's approach was "so sensitive, so honest, so *sweet*" that it totally unnerved her. "I can't tell you how *sexy*, how warm it made me feel toward Tim," she said.

Can you understand that?

I'm not sure I can. I grew up thinking that women only liked suave, debonair, self-assured men. Now they're telling me they also like vulnerability, awkwardness, shyness. So be it. Who am I to quibble with reality, particularly when it turns out to be a more generous, more *accepting* reality than I anticipated?

In short, perhaps it's high time to stop thinking of shyness as a drawback, a liability, and to start realizing that it may actually be an asset, a pickup technique that can work *for* you rather than against you.

Give it a try. Next time you're at a bar or a party and you spot a woman who knocks you out, walk up and say, "Um, usually I'm much too shy to introduce myself to a woman I don't know, but I feel I've just got to meet you." That's all. And don't worry if you cluck or stutter or think you appear nervous as hell. In many cases that can be a plus. The woman will feel you're genuine, not just trying to rack up yet another easy score.

Of course if you're too shy to try the above, I doubt that any amount of encouragement on my part is going to do the trick. You're probably going to stand around, night after night, slugging down beer after beer, trying somehow to get up the courage to talk to a girl, knowing in your heart you won't. I suspect what's going to happen to you finally is that some young wench will walk up, ask what's your sign, and you'll be so damn grateful that *you* didn't have to do any of the work that you'll marry her. That's what usually happens to shy guys, you know. They marry the first girl that comes along, which in the long run may be all fine and good but certainly puts a crimp in sowing one's wild oats. I can't tell you how many middle-aged guys I've run into, now no longer shy, who curse their fate for not having had the guts to wade right into that pool of long-legged young lovelies that was available to them back when they were carefree and single.

But what can I do about it, Eric? I'm just hopelessly shy. I could no more walk up to a girl I don't know than I could beat out Lawrence Taylor for a linebacker slot on the New York Giants.

Well, don't despair. Following you'll find several techniques for meeting women that are so risk free, so mild, so nonthreatening to your ego, that I think even the shyest guy on Earth could give them a try without going through a trauma. So here they are, guys, my special nonverbal techniques for meeting women. They may not be quite so effective as walking up and saying, "Hi, my name is Joe," but according to all my research, both theoretical and in the field, they're a pretty good second best.

SMILE. *Smile!? That's the dumbest idea you've ever had, Weber. She'll see the gap between my front teeth.*

Listen, I don't care if you've got a piece of spinach lodged between your front teeth. Short of a clear, firm hello, a smile is about the best signal you can send a woman. Most guys think smiling is feminine or fruity or nerdy. Women tell me just the opposite. A smile, they say, is sexy. Men look more erotic when they smile, more accessible, more touchable.

Perhaps you've grown up on a diet of Clint Eastwood movies—you know, sucked-in cheeks and scowls and sneers. That may be okay if you're six feet six inches tall and can bench press five trillion kilos. But on the average man a smile is vastly more inviting and attractive than the tough-guy look. First of all, it can be frightening to a woman to have you glare at her like you want to punch her out. Second, why communicate hostility when what you really feel is warmth and probably a touch of lust? Women like it when you want them. It flatters their egos. It makes them like you back.

Of course, the best thing about smiling is that it's something a shy guy can do without a lot of work, planning, or psyching himself up. You just draw back the corners of your mouth and grin. *You* may feel you look silly this way, but as I said earlier, women like it. You look friendlier and quite possibly handsomer. Many women will feel motivated to smile back, if not out of horniness for you at least in the spirit of one human being greeting another. If she does that, you almost can't help but say hello. And just like that you can be launched into a conversation—no risk, no terror, no bumbling and stuttering, no having to walk across a crowded singles bar only to have her shoot you down.

So don't just sit there nodding in agreement as you read, thinking to yourself, *Not a bad idea. I'll have to give that a try.* Get out there and actually do it. Smile at women on the street, on public transportation like buses and trains, in elevators, at school, or at work. It doesn't have to be a giant, goofy smile like out of a Colgate ad . . . just a little nod and a smile, as if in greeting. You'll be astonished at how many women return your greeting. (Women tell me that men hardly ever smile at them and that they love it when one does.) After that, starting a conversation becomes a thousand times easier.

And I'm not going to let you hide behind the excuse that smiling is old hat . . . every guy does it. The truth is, I hardly ever see a man who smiles at the women he encounters . . . and the few men I *do* see smile usually seem to have rather crowded love lives. So smile. As they say, smiling takes 487 (or something like that) fewer facial muscles than frowning.

SEND A NOTE. Here's another way to start a relationship with a girl you're too afraid to address in person. Drop her a note telling her how you feel—not a grief-stricken love letter, just something light, like, "Dear Eileen, I'm a bit on the shy side, so I'm taking pen in hand to tell you I think there's something very special about you and I'd like to get to know you. Best, Ben."

You can use my very words, if you like (changing the last word, of course, if your name is Derek or Lloyd). I won't guarantee they'll work every time, but I will suggest that they'll work a hell of a lot better than not doing anything at all.

I know many shy guys who swear by this technique . . . and many women have told me that they'd be thrilled to get a note like the one above. I have also seen cards in card shops which are meant to serve as letters of introduction, and some of them are very clever—far cleverer, in fact, than most of us would be if left to our own devices. So if you have trouble putting into words what is in your heart, let Hallmark do it for you.

Again, this is a doable idea that you could put into practice just five minutes after putting this book down. So don't let it go to waste. It works.

SEND A BOTTLE OF WINE. Like the smile, sending a woman a drink may be a bit old-fashioned and clichéd, but how do you suppose it got that way? Because it works, knucklehead. That's how ideas *become* clichés. They are so effective that people learn to rely on them when they can't think of anything new or unique. Kind of like those god-awful, real-people testimonial commercials. Apparently they're almost always effective.

And so is sending a woman a drink. Everyone's heard about it, but when was the last time you saw a man actually go ahead and do it? Bet you can't remember. But that doesn't mean it's not worth a try. The worst that'll happen is that it'll cost you five bucks, and all you'll get from her in return is a polite nod of the head and a smile. Certainly that's better than being overlooked altogether.

On the other hand, many women are so delighted when they're sent a drink that they can't help but be drawn to the fellow who was thoughtful, courtly, and generous enough to do it.

And finally, it's something that any shy man can do since it doesn't involve even looking a girl in the eye. You just call your waiter over (bartender in a bar), and ask what the slim brunette at the corner table is drinking. Then direct him to bring her another, or, if you want to really impress her, a split (that's a half bottle) of wine or champagne. In most cases the waiter will be only too happy to oblige. Everybody loves a lover.

USE FRIENDLY INTRODUCTIONS. Many of us, particularly those who are really shy, will conceal from our closest friends that we have a crush on someone. For example, there's a new girl in your math class or at the branch where you bank. You find yourself falling head over heels for her, fantasizing about her day and night. But tell anybody? You'd rather be dead.

The question is . . . Why? Are you aware that when it comes to meeting new women your friends can often help you more than you can help yourself. After all, if they don't have a crush on the same girl you do and they're fearless about approaching women, you can often get them to do the hard part for you.

Let's say you work as a mechanic in a garage. Every once in a while a girl in a white convertible Mustang drives in to chat with the guy who pumps gas, who just happens to be a good buddy of yours. Seems like he and the girl are old friends. Why not approach him, tell him you'd really like to meet the girl with the Mustang, and ask him to introduce you? No big deal. Unless it's his wife or fiancée, most likely he'll be only too glad to lend a hand. Like I said, the world loves love and romance. And people particularly like to be there at its inception, so they can say a dozen years later, "And I was the one who introduced them."

And I don't care how shy you are. If your pal calls you over to meet Elizabeth, it's certainly easier than walking up to her yourself and saying, "Didn't you go to Memorial High?"

So lean on your friends. That's what they're there for.

Well, that's my system for meeting women if you're too shy to walk straight up and introduce yourself—smile, send a note, send a drink, have a friend introduce you. They all work . . . and I think that they'll feel comfortable and executable, something you can attempt without getting so keyed up you feel like you're going to faint. And remember, girls *want* you to approach them, even if your approach is as awkward as a right-hander bowling lefty. So go for it. You'll be amazed at your success, even if I'm not surprised in the least.

5

How to Get Women to Pick You Up

My neighbors have a two-year-old son. He toddles into the kitchen while his mother is making dinner, sidles up close, raises his arms beseechingly in the air, and says with astonishing clarity these very words: "Mommy, pick me up."

I'll bet when you were a little boy, you did the same. In fact, who among us has not?

It has its advantages, this ancient Oedipal ritual . . . and it has its flaws.

To have our big, soft, warm, cuddly mother pick us up and hug us to her breast instills in us, when we need it most, a sense of being lovable, adored, wanted. This can help us with women as we grow older. I'm sure you have a friend who automatically assumes all women will like him, whether he's at the beach, at work, or lolling on a blanket at a concert in the park. And who doesn't have such a friend? Somehow his mother did such a good job of implanting in him a sense of being loved and desirable that he has carried these feelings into adulthood. He may not be particularly bright, rich, good-looking, or even interesting, yet women are drawn to him, swept into his path of self-love as naturally, well, as naturally as a mother picking up her baby boy.

The *problem* with your mother's picking you up is that it can also lead to a certain passivity, a longing to have women go on picking you up for the rest of your life. Think of all the times you've sat around in singles bars and discotheques hoping for a miracle, attempting to *will* that pretty straw-haired creature across the room to come over and talk to you or ask you to dance. The most frightening and counterproductive aspect of this fantasy is that in part of our brain we actually believe it *can* happen . . . that just as our mother occasionally scooped us up with a burst of affection, beautiful strangers may sometimes do the same.

I have good news and bad news for you.

The bad news is that it ain't likely to happen very often, particularly if you plod along as you usually do, ignoring much of the advice that follows. For no matter what you hear about women's lib and ERA and modern women, the fact is that most women still don't see *their* doing the picking up as a glamorous, feminine, romantic act. Men do. They fantasize about it and admire those men who are skilled at it. For some men it defines their sense of self. *I can pick up women; therefore, I am a superior man.* Witness the sales of two of the books I've created. *How to Pick Up Girls* has sold two million copies and has been translated into Japanese, French, Spanish, Portuguese, Greek, and German. *How to Pick Up Men* (for women) has not yet sold 200,000 copies. Thus one could say that for every ten men who want to pick up women, only one woman wants to pick up a man —not exactly auspicious odds.

And yet—now for the good news—life in America *is* changing. *Slowly,* but it's changing. More women are starting to pick up more men. I see evidence of it nearly everywhere. The other evening I was having dinner at one of those restaurant cum singles bars, where the serious eaters sit at tables on one side of the establishment and those looking to get laid, or at least meet people, mill about the bar on the other side. Over a period of not more than two hours I made three separate and distinct sightings of women hitting up on men: (1) from an executive type in her early thirties to a man in a suit, "Don't you work for Bristol-Myers?" (2) a collegiate-looking girl to a large, blocky young man in a crew-neck sweater, "Hi! I'm Kathy. What's your name?" (3) a sultry woman in her early forties walking up to a lad easily twenty years her junior, "Do you have a light?"

Granted, the men in the room were even more assertive. But then I doubt that ten years ago, or even five, I would have spotted *any* such brazen female-initiated pickups.

Now if this happened in less than half an evening in one singles bar in one medium-sized city, and on a lackluster Wednesday night, no less, imagine how many times this will happen next weekend across the country as a whole. Probably well over half a million women, some of them spectacularly sexy and witty and long-legged and fascinating and high-bosomed, are going to try to pick up a man. And why shouldn't you be one of those lucky guys they're going after?

Well, there's no reason. But to sit around and *prepare* yourself to be picked up is passive. It doesn't lead to growth. In my experience, it is only those people who are willing to take risks and to hold themselves open for rejection and ridicule who grow, become great, and rise above ordinary mortals. That caveat raised, I now plunge ahead to tell you exactly how to get women to pick you up.

I realize that while there may be a few of you out there who are interested in being great, in boldly taking the world by storm, letting the chips fall where they will, most men are looking to do things with as little risk, as little work, as little pain, and as much fun and reward as possible.

And with life being as tricky, ruthless, and perilous as it is, who can blame them? So on to getting picked up.

In an earlier part of this book I recommended that men who want to meet girls take yoga lessons. What I didn't mention is that it is an even better place to give women the chance to meet you. The wonderful thing about yoga class is that there is rarely competition from other men, and the occasional guy you do run into is more than likely to be gay. So picture this. Here you are in a cozy little wood-floored studio with six, nine, a dozen women all in tight, skimpy leotards. You are stretching and bending and grunting and reaching together. Your feet and hips and hands are in their face, their buttocks and bosoms and shoulders in yours. The parallels between this and real lovemaking are awesome. And generally these aren't your average run-of-the-mill women but those who are interested in their body, in keeping it lean and trim and in shape. And women who are interested in their body are by extension interested in their face and hair and overall appearance. So in yoga class you're likely to run into some extremely comely girls. One acquaintance, a psychiatrist, says that he followed my advice and wound up marrying the teacher, a stunning woman in her late twenties.

Now how do you get them to pick you up? Just by being there, by going through the motions, just as your female classmates are. It is important not to act like a fox in a chicken coop, licking your lips in anticipation of an imminent feast. Simply pretend you are interested in yoga or in getting or staying in shape. Don't race around asking the prettiest creatures there to join you after class for a magnum of wine. Don't collect telephone numbers. Don't wink and leer at anyone who happens to look at you. Try to project a look of innocence, of nonchalance. All the delicious-looking bodies being flashed about mean little to you. You are only here for the exercise, for the sheer pleasure of yoga. Remember?

Well, then, how the hell am I going to get anywhere with these scrumptious-looking exercisers if I don't make my intentions known? By doing nothing! For what is going to happen, surely as I am sitting here typing, is this: Sooner or later one of your classmates is going to take notice of you. After all, you're a man. And even if you're a fairly ordinary one, the odds are that at least one of the dozen or so women in the room is going to be at least mildly attracted to you. And that's all it will take. It may not be until your third or fourth class, but soon you'll find her lining up next to you, smiling at you, even saying hi to you. She may linger after class and chat about the weather or ask you questions about what you do, where you live, and how it is you're taking yoga.

Now when this happens, the normal reaction of most men is to respond with alacrity, with too much eager enthusiasm. I know it may not be easy, but play it cool. Act polite, but don't go overboard and propose a lunch date, an evening at the theater, a vacation in the Bahamas together, or marriage. Don't even ask for her telephone number—yet. Because what you want to happen is for some of the other women to notice what's going on. If you think men are competitive when a lone woman enters the room, watch what happens when women begin fighting for the same man. Pearl Harbor revisited! Even those who were not originally attracted to you will jump into the fray. Before you know it, it will be *they* who are suggesting drinks, dates, and your coming over to their place for dinner. Why, you'll be able to take your pick, or schedule a different one for every night of the week.

All this notwithstanding, I realize, of course, that some of you may still be just a little too inhibited to slip into a pair of tights and stretch into some weird Far East position. So don't. Take a dance exercise class, regular ballroom, or disco lessons. If you become a truly superb dancer, don't be surprised to find women asking *you* to dance. Or if dancing just isn't your thing, take a course in French, pottery, or ceramics. There are dozens of areas of interest that seem to bring great bodies of women together with almost no attendant men. And if you want women to pick you up, that's where you ought to be.

To make it even *easier* for the women at hand to approach you, I suggest the following: Wear something that invites conversation. A save-the-whales button. A shirt that identifies your school, fraternity, or a ten-thousand-kilometer race you've run. Carry a controversial book or magazine. Bring along a camera, poster, or painting you've just bought. Ride a bicycle or wear roller skates to class. Do anything you can think of—so long as you're not being too show-offy or exhibitionistic—that will make it natural, and thus comfortable, for a woman to comment on. Don't forget, picking up men is still new to women, even the most avant-garde of them, and the more matter-of-fact and acceptable you can make it for them, the quicker they're going to pick you up.

How else can you get women to pick you up?

If you're young and carefree enough and have the summer off, I suggest applying for a job as a cabana or pool boy or as a lifeguard (if you swim well enough) at a country club. During the day, while the men work, their wives and daughters bake. And when women are lying around in nothing but a skimpy bathing suit, heating up under the blazing sun, admiring their own tan limbs and lithe bodies, their minds inevitably turn to sex. And who can supply that better than the nice man who is bringing them their tall, cool gin and tonic—you.

Another technique is to spend a day or two doing research at an all-woman's, or nearly all-woman's, college or university. The most famous ones, such as Smith and Mount Holyoke, are in the Northeast, but such schools exist all over the country. Find out what schools are located in your area and what the ratio of women to men is. Any institution with a nursing program is almost guaranteed to have a disproportionate number of women, regardless of whether it's an all-woman's school or not.

Or, if you can't find such a place near you, just go to any library and walk around as if you were lost. Ever notice that most librarians are female? And you never know what may happen when one takes you behind the stacks.

One of the most surefire ways to get yourself picked up is to go to a beautician to get your hair cut. Some men do this because they can get a better haircut, and you can just claim —if anybody nosy asks—that appearance is a very crucial part of your job. Beauty shops are packed with women of all different ages with one thing in common—they care about looking beautiful. On top of this, many of the women who spend time there are quite rich and often bored. They'd like nothing better than to start a conversation with a well-groomed fellow such as yourself.

In short, my friends, go where there are lots and lots of women and as few men as possible. Do it, and I assure you that at least some of them, and maybe a whole bunch of them, will wind up being just as big a pushover as your mother once was.

6

Why a Man Doesn't Have to Be Good-looking

Before we proceed further with the technique—the real nuts and bolts of meeting, wooing, and winning with women—I think it is essential to deal with some of the fears that seem to keep many a good man from partaking in as active a social and sex life as he would like. It makes little sense to show you how to take a woman out on a splendid date if you're too afraid to call her in the first place.

This is not to say that I can give you total confidence in your ability to attract women or that I can teach you how to love your own looks. Feelings of self-esteem ebb and flow, partly because of events in your outer life and partly because of internal rhythms governed by the real bedrock inner you. What I can do, however, is allay some of your most common fears and misconceptions about what women want and demonstrate to you that women are much warmer and more accepting and eager to meet you than you probably realize. And once you know that, I think you'll find yourself much braver and more confident around them, which is often all it takes to improve your success with the opposite sex dramatically.

Whenever I give my New York City seminar on how to meet new women, some guy in the back of the room invariably raises his hand and asks, "Yeah, but doesn't a guy have to be good-looking?"

The question usually sets off an undercurrent of sympathetic murmurs and whispers. The speaker has dared to ask the unaskable, has spoken aloud the one major fear playing in the back of everyone's mind: *Will women find me attractive?*

I must confess, I'm tempted at these times to answer, "Yes, you're probably right, a fellow has to look exactly like O. J. Simpson or Robert Redford or he'll never find a woman, and since none of you guys, or me for the matter, even remotely resembles a handsome movie star, let's pack up our bags and call it quits or sign up for a life term at a monastery."

Of course, I don't respond this way at all. I try to be thoughtful and sympathetic. For what the speaker is really getting at, I suspect, is this: *Next to some of my friends I don't feel very attractive at all. On Friday night a bunch of us will go out to a singles bar together, and while I'm standing around checking out the girls, trying to get up the courage to approach one, I can see that the girls are all checking out my friend Nick or Sam, not even giving me a second glance. Sometimes, girls will come right up to Nick or Sam and pick them up, without their ever having to say anything at all. I get the average girls (if I get any at all) and my pals get the beauties, and they don't even have to work for them. It's not fair.*

Damn right it's not fair. Life isn't fair. Some people are born with looks or money or brains or the ability to play second base . . . or, even more frustrating, some are born with a whole multitude of advantages, none of them earned or deserved or fought for. So what are you going to do? Give up and roll over and wait until you're reincarnated as

Christopher Reeve? Or are you going to decide, *Well, so I wasn't born the handsomest stud on two legs. Ain't nothing I can do about that. But I am a nice, friendly, good-hearted guy who could give a great-looking woman the evening of a lifetime, and perhaps the lifetime of a lifetime, if only she'd give me a chance.*

That's all it takes to win a superior woman, you know, the simple belief that if you and she were snowbound in a log cabin for two weeks with a case of wine and a good stereo system, she'd wind up having one hell of a time. It doesn't matter if you're not particularly good-looking (and I'm not willing to concede yet that you're not, since men are often their own most severe and mistaken critics), or even if you don't have any confidence in your looks at all. The only thing that really counts is that you have some kind of trust or confidence in your personality, your soul, your inner humanity. For after initial attractions, it is what is inside you more than anything else that determines the intensity with which women will be drawn to you. And if you're the kind of guy who's always walked around feeling, *Damn, if girls could only see beyond faces they'd be nuts about me,* then I believe you're the kind of guy who can win just about any woman you want. All it takes is a little patience, a little risk-taking, and a little rethinking. But, hell, to a guy like you, that's nothing.

7

How to Tell
When a Woman Likes
You

I address this subject with mixed feelings. Partly I am filled
with eager enthusiasm, a sense of delectation, for I know of
no other feeling quite as thrilling or heady as that which
occurs when you begin to pick up the subtle but unmistak-
able signs that a beautiful new woman is developing a crush
on you. The simple act of writing about it is enough to
make me feel as if it's happening right now—the gaze that
lingers a touch too long (and yet not nearly long enough),
the unexpected touch upon one's arm, the slight tilting of
her head as she listens with admiring eyes.

On the other hand, I have misgivings. Will too many of
my readers come away disappointed? *If those are the signals
women send out to men they like, no one's flashing any at me. I knew
women didn't like me! I might as well give up.*

Before we even begin, I want to make it very clear that (a)

many of the signs women send out are so subtle you may be missing them altogether, and (b) even if you're correct in thinking that no women are at present pursuing you, that doesn't mean you can't become a winner with women anyway. Who says a woman has to like you first? I know scores of men who have developed the technique of attracting uninterested women, of starting loving relationships with women who for a while had totally overlooked them.

So let's not consign ourselves to a life of celibacy just because no woman as yet has batted her eyes at us. In future chapters we'll be discussing dozens of ways to turn the ladies' heads your way, if they're not doing enough of that already. Right now, though, let's just concentrate on learning what the signals are that a woman sends out to let you know she likes you. I maintain that if you become skilled at that, you'll discover there are more women who are attracted to you, who want to go out with you, than you ever could have fantasized.

Does She Laugh at Your Jokes?

Of all the women I interviewed on this subject, well over half said they try very hard to laugh at a man's jokes. "This may sound terrible," says a lovely-looking New York City fashion consultant, "but I crack up over jokes that I don't even think are funny." This, by the way, is a sophisticated, liberated woman, one I never would have dreamed in these times of honesty and equality would have compromised herself just for the sake of wooing a man. Old customs die hard indeed.

So if you come across a woman who seems unusually responsive to your brand of humor, ask yourself this: *Is there more here than meets the eye?* Perhaps you thought you were being just plain funny. Maybe she's trying to tell you something else.

Does She Touch You?

This is a surefire sign that a woman is warming up to you, and I don't care how convinced you are that women do it merely out of friendship or mild affection. I've been doing a study on touching for over a decade now, and the one thing I've noticed is this: Women who are touchers *never* touch a man they're not interested in and *always* find plenty of excuses to touch a man whom they are attracted to. Touching, for women in particular, seems to be a form of ritualized behavior to attract the opposite sex.

"I'm a very physical person," Suzanne, a Chicago stockbroker, told me.

"Yes, but do you ever touch a man you're not attracted to?"

"Never."

"And what about men you like?"

"Constantly. I can't seem to help myself. I do it without thinking about it."

Think about it yourself. Is there a woman at work or school or one who is a part of your crowd who occasionally touches your shoulder, your arm, or your hand? I'll bet she likes you, possibly more than you ever realized.

Does She Really Listen to You?

A writer I know from Long Island, an attractive woman in her early thirties, claims there isn't a woman's magazine in the country that goes a year without featuring an article on how important being a good listener is in attracting a man. "Women grow up on that advice," she says. "If they're not good listeners to begin with, they pretend they are."

Keep that in mind the next time you're at a party, a dance, or a singles bar. If all of a sudden you find someone staring at you with rapt attention as you prattle on about your heroics in a weekend softball game, don't assume it's merely because she finds softball so fascinating. More likely, it's *you* she finds fascinating. And if her eyes seem moist and dewy as she listens, then you can be *sure* she finds you fascinating. Scientists claim that getting dewy-eyed is an involuntary reaction that women have when they look at a man they're strongly attracted to.

Does She Stand Close to You?

There have been so many articles and books on the meaning of crossed arms and uncrossed legs in recent years that I hesitate to add my humble observations. Suffice it to say that if you feel a woman's *nearness,* if you get vibrations that she is leaning toward you, facing you directly, then she is probably trying to tell you something.

As an experiment, study the people in a restaurant or at a party. Notice at whom the different women have their knees and chests pointed. Even if they temporarily turn their eyes and heads to someone who is speaking, it is the person at whom they have their body directed who they are feeling the most warmth toward. Look for women whose bodies are turned to you. They're interested.

Does She Gaze at You?

This is another surefire sign. Almost every woman I interviewed said she tries to establish "lots of eye contact" with a man she's interested in. Have you ever found yourself playing "eyesies" with a girl on a bus or at a singles bar and thought, *No, it can't be. My fly must be open. She's looking at someone in back of me. I remind her of her Uncle Harry.* Wrong. She's giving you one of the strongest, most obvious signals she can. Walk up and say, "Hi. You look nice." That's all you have to do to start the ball rolling.

Is She Friendly?

I can't tell you how many men attribute simple friendliness to a woman's outgoing nature. *Oh, she's just being friendly.* Nonsense. She's being seductive. As a stewardess from Denver told me, "Who's got time to be friendly to everyone you meet? Mind you, I'm cordial to strangers, but I save my genuine warmth and friendliness for men I'm really interested in. I don't ask, 'Did you have a nice flight?' unless I want to start a conversation with a man."

Is there a woman at work who always asks, "Did you have a good weekend?" or a waitress at a diner who asks, "How was your day?" Don't be so sure it's just because they're good-natured. See what happens when you try to take the conversation a little further—to the point, for example, where you suggest having a drink after work. Generally women don't feel free enough to make so direct an overture. So they do the next best thing. They act friendly. Take them up on it. Watch how really friendly the two of you can get.

Is She Giving You Vibrations?

When I look back over the years, I can recall dozens of little fleeting exchanges with women—in coffee lines, in elevators, at bus stops, etc.—in which a little magic was occurring, but I was too slow to pick up on it. "Nice day." "Nice tie." "That danish looks delicious." "The bus is late again," they'd say. I'd sense their interest but wouldn't feel enough urgency to keep the conversation going. But an hour later, or sometimes a *year* later, a powerful thought would flash into mind. *That woman liked me!* Most of the time it was too late to do anything about it.

Don't let this happen to you. Seemingly petty little exchanges at newsstands, at lunch counters, in supermarket lines, and in apartment lobbies are often vastly more significant than you realize at the time. If you got a smile, a hello, a nod, a good morning, that didn't happen by accident. The woman was drawn to you enough to extend herself, to send out a feeler; and if you're so inclined, I would urge you to follow up on it.

For example, if you're at the express counter at the A&P, and the woman behind you mutters, "What's taking so long?" (a perfect example of the previously mentioned all-natural approach), perhaps you should use her remark as a springboard to launch a full-scale conversation. It's easy enough for you to respond, "It's always like this. Do you shop here often?"

You'll be astonished at how many more relationships you might find yourself in if you tried turning these brief encounters into more extended ones, rather than just letting them evaporate into the atmosphere.

Does She Always Seem to Be Around?

In response to the question "How do you let a man know you like him?" a pretty young paralegal replied, "I stick out my tits, suck in my stomach, and walk by his desk twenty times a day. But I never make the first move. I always try to get him to notice me so that he makes the first move."

What's the moral here? If you suddenly begin to notice a woman, it may be because she's planned it that way. Perhaps you thought the reason the girl at the next table kept on getting up to go to the ladies' room was that she'd drunk too much beer. Or that the secretary from downstairs was using the Xerox machine outside your office because the one on her floor was broken. Or that the girl in the next apartment simply walks her dog the same time you do because it's convenient.

Maybe not. Maybe the real reason they seem to be popping up in your life with increasing frequency is that they're trying to get you to notice them. Often, women who use this approach are shy and hide behind a mask of indifference, lest you get the idea that they're after you. But after you they may be. So think about it. Is there a woman out there you seem constantly to be bumping into by happenstance? Smile and say hi. I'll bet she's only too glad you finally stopped to notice.

What I'm trying to impress upon you here is that all day long women are sending out an infinite number and variety of signals to men, signals that are often a good deal more meaningful than they seem. Obviously, most women don't feel free enough—yet, anyway—to walk up and say, "I think you have great legs," or, "What are you doing Friday night?" Society has taught them that they must be subtler, less assertive, more discreet in their advances.

Unfortunately, some of them are so discreet that if we're not really concentrating, we overlook the signals or misinterpret them as mere courtesy.

My advice to you is that you step out into the world today with all your antennae working; and that if the pretty blonde at the dry-cleaning store smiles at you as she hands you your slacks, you make damn sure what she meant by it before you go traipsing out of there, cursing your fate because women don't seem to take to you. One of the women I talked with summed up the situation succinctly: "I guess I've been conditioned to make all my overtures passive ones. I smile, I act friendly, I try to look pretty and sexy, for men to notice me. I would say that of every one hundred signals I send out, a man takes me up on maybe only three or four of them. It's very frustrating."

8

Those First Five Minutes

Hallelujah!

I'm going to assume that you've tried one or more of the strategies from the previous section and that lo and behold you've actually met a woman. Well, you've sort of met a woman. So far, you've *addressed* a woman, caught up with her at the punch bowl, and blurted out, "D-d-d-d-don't I know you from somewhere?"

Now you've got a problem. Instead of responding, "Yes, let's fuck," or, "No, thank God," she's simply stared at you curiously and said, "I don't know. Maybe."

You weren't expecting this. In all of your ruminating and scheming about approaching a woman, you'd always thought that you'd either get bopped over the head with her purse or dragged onto the nearest mattress for some quick and hungry lovemaking—fast, violent, conclusive stuff, nothing lukewarm or in-between.

Now, horror of horrors, you've actually got to stand

there and talk to her, make words come out of your mouth, which is something you may not be prepared for. In fact, if you're like most guys, you've probably devoted ninety percent of your energy to getting up the courage to deliver an opening line and hardly any thought at all about what comes after it. And that's a mistake. Almost anything can work as a conversation opener, from "Let me see your papers" to "Hi, my name's Biff." The real art comes in sustaining conversation, in starting a dialogue between you and her that builds to a harmonious, passionate, symphonic pitch.

If all of this seems somehow overwhelming, don't despair. Over the past dozen years I've done a fair amount of experimental field-testing in the area. And I've found the following shortcuts to intimacy to be rather effective— sometimes, in fact, almost *frighteningly* effective.

Of course, I don't expect all, or even the majority, of them to be perfect for you. But, then, when it comes to enriching your love life, one idea is all it takes.

Find Someone Who Turns You On

When I was in high school, there was a girl in my class that just about every boy in the place had a crush on. In fact, so powerful was the group attraction toward Jean that I thought I had a crush on her, too. The curious thing, though, was that whenever I had a sex fantasy—at sixteen, I had a fair number—they were never about sweet Jean at all. Instead they featured a far less pretty girl who was my lab partner in biology. Although her nose was much bigger than Jean's and her bosom far smaller, there was something cute about Ann, something that moved me.

Nevertheless, I strutted and preened for Jean like all the other guys, daydreaming what a coup it would be to show up at the Turkey Trot with her on my arm. Ann I paid little attention to—my friend Charlie quipped she had a face like a truck driver's—except, of course, in my nocturnal thrashings. What a fool I was. To this day I remember the feel of her pert little breasts pressing against my back as she peered over my shoulder, the better to watch me slice open our poor, wrinkled frog. The pleasure I felt when I was with her! The good times we could have had!

The point is that if you really want to progress beyond the opening line, you must pick out a girl who genuinely moves you, not one who is *supposed* to move you, not one whom your friend has described as dynamite but you find rather blah. Because if you're not really interested in a woman and have approached her only because it seems like a good idea, she'll sense it in minutes. And that's when your relationship will end—in minutes. She'll excuse herself to freshen her makeup and that'll be the last you see of her. You'll be left standing at the punch bowl, alone, feeling rejected and defeated. And for what? The truth is, you didn't really want her in the first place. No wonder your conversation didn't have any zip and your smile was void of life. But that's okay. There are a couple of hundred million other girls to choose from. This time pick one who really turns you on, one you're drawn to, one whose eyes or voice or aura attracts you as well as her pretty face. You'll be thrilled at how much more energy and desire you feel, how much more appetite you have for the chase. And she'll sense it, too. And that'll make all the difference in the world.

Hang in There

The temptation of most men, upon finding out that their job is not done as soon as they deliver their opening line, is to flee. It's as if they'd just punched some big bruiser in a bar fight who, instead of going down, had simply blinked and grunted. The advice here is don't flee. Just stand there. Your silence is neither as awkward nor as strange as you might think. Letting a minute or two go by without ticking off a string of familiar questions says some pretty good things about you: You're not a blabbermouth; you expect her to talk, too; you didn't rehearse your approach ahead of time (even if you really did).

Furthermore she, as well as you, will feel an urge to fill the void. Maybe she'll think of something to say before you do. That, of course, will solve your problem of not having thought of anything else but your opening line.

The important thing to remember is this: Don't panic. Don't run away. Remember, you're the strong silent type. Simply take a deep breath and hang in there. Smile. Hum. Study the crowd. If you can do that, you'll be a giant step ahead of your competitors, most of whom will back off at the first hint of a lull in the conversation, interpreting it as a sign that the girl they've approached doesn't like them. That's often far from the truth. Unless a man looks like Richard Gere or Quasimodo, chances are the girl doesn't know yet whether or not she likes him. She's got to spend some time talking with him, which leads us to our next step.

Don't Be Afraid to Say Something Trite

What has made approaching a woman such a fearsome bugaboo in many men's minds is the mistaken belief that it can only be accomplished with dialogue that is clever, witty, disarming. After all, that's how it's done in movies. You never hear Cary Grant say, "Excuse me, but didn't you sit next to me in business math in Kenosha High?"

The cinema notwithstanding, the reality is that every week millions of women are drawn into conversation with chatter that could make a Shriner yawn. "Nice weather for ducks." "Is there a post office around here?" "Who do you like in the Preakness?"

Maybe clichés are not your style, but the next time you're

in the process of chatting with a woman and the dark cloud of silence starts to settle down around you, give one a try. Better yet, come armed with one or two. For example, if it was a rainy day, declare (ironically), "Great day today, huh?" She'll probably respond something like this: "I'll say. I got absolutely soaked on the way home from work. And wouldn't you know I forgot my umbrella . . ."

Naturally, you don't want to go on this way all evening long, or even for five minutes if you can help it. But if the pressure of the situation has you momentarily tongue-tied, don't think you're going to blow it by saying the first trite thing that comes to mind. Contrary to Shakespeare, life is not played out on a stage, but in elevators with Hawaiian music pumped in and in finished basements with checkerboard floors. And saying something ordinary may just trigger enough conversation on her part to buy you the time for your true, dazzling self to come to the surface.

Be Nice

A lot of men feel that to be nice to a woman is to be weak, to appear desperate . . . that it's a dead giveaway that you're attracted to her.

It's a sign that you're attracted to her, all right. But what on Earth could be wrong with that? Men may not be aware of it, but women certainly are: *A truly confident man isn't shy in the least about letting a woman know he wants to spend time with her.* He feels good about his attraction to her. He expects her to be *flattered* by his interest in her. And in most cases she will be.

Women don't think you're being weak by being nice. They think you're being strong. So if you feel an impulse to tell her she has beautiful skin, soulful eyes, a classic nose, a sensuous voice, a pretty name, do it. And use her name often. It's flattering and assures her you're talking to her and not just to any woman. Tell her you're having a good time conversing with her, that she's different from other girls, more interesting, more fun to be with. Be creative. Tell her she's statuesque, Romanesque, Latinesque, whatever's appropriate.

Now your pal across the room, he still thinks it's cool to act like Charles Bronson. Mean. Quiet. To snarl. To insult. Know what? That kind of behavior went out with the forties, if it was ever in in the first place. Oh, sure, some women like tough guys, mean guys. About one in ten are like that and want a man who will push them around, punish them, cheat on them, hit them. And that's fine. But you don't want a woman like that. You want a healthy woman. And healthy women like men who will treat them nicely, with respect, with tenderness. Just one caution. Don't use this as an excuse to go to pieces, to break down altogether and haul out your package of woes.

Oh, Deirdre, you're so beautiful, so lovely. You don't know how lonely I've been living at home with my mother, dreaming that one day a girl like you would come along and rescue me from my misery. How kind you are to shed your light on a pathetic, unemployable creep such as I.

Unless you've accidentally bumped into a latent Florence Nightingale, that kind of crap'll get you nowhere. Fast. To be nice doesn't mean to be fawning or obsequious. It simply means having the confidence to verbalize your feelings of warmth and generosity toward the wonderful creature you've just met, to tell her she makes you feel good, to get her a drink from the bar, to offer her your jacket to combat the overly zealous air-conditioning.

So if you're basically a nice guy, don't hide it. Your niceness is one of your greatest attractions. Let the other guys lurk against the wall trying to look like they're in the mob. You'll get the girl, and they'll go home by themselves. Come to think of it, no wonder they look so cranky and mean.

Make Her Feel Special

Implicit in much of the preceding advice is that it's important to make a woman feel special. To tell you the truth, it's something that had never occurred to me before I'd written *How to Pick Up Girls*. I had always assumed that women wanted men who were rich, debonair, impossibly good-looking, even if it meant having to put up with someone who was self-absorbed and narcissistic. But the women I interviewed for *How to Pick Up Girls* impressed upon me that they are far more interested in men who know how to make them feel good about themselves than in men who have everything but graciousness and consideration for others. If a man makes a woman feel beautiful, interesting, *superior,* then it's not so important for him to be superior himself. Is that perfectly clear? How you make a woman feel about herself is pretty much how she will come to feel about you. If you make her feel that she's unique, then she will decide that you are unique. So tell her. "There's something special about you. I noticed you the second I walked in the room. You have a very unique voice, unusual, different. I can't explain it. You're more than just pretty. There's something very original about your looks."

And don't let it slip your mind. Before you go out tonight, commit the following to memory: *There's something special about you.* Then don't be afraid to use it. At the first sign of a lull in the conversation, say, "I don't know, Susan, but there's something special about you." Watch how she smiles and lights up. And, of course, if you've followed my advice about finding someone you're genuinely attracted to, then your compliment will be equally genuine. You really will think she's special.

9

How to Warm Her Up

Okay, your conversation is proceeding with moderate success. You and she are now talking up a storm about the hors d'oeuvres, how good they are, how lousy they are, how cholesterol is the root of all evil, what have you. It is time to pick the relationship up and carry it bodily to a more intimate plane. Now, for most guys, this ain't easy. I remember myself in the early stages prattling on for hours about my job, her job, politics, everything I didn't want to talk about, nothing that I did want to talk about, as if I were caught in a rondo and didn't know how to get out.

I wanted to have fun, laugh, talk sexy, kiss, hug, dance, and get stoned, and instead I sounded more and more like a lawyer reading aloud the contract at a house closing. I can't tell you how many terrific-looking girls I bored into keeping on their pants. Then I discovered an amazing question: "Do you model?"

Preposterous, you say? *Only a girl with an IQ under 75* (in

which case you don't want her anyway) *would believe a come-
on like that?*

You just try it. I personally guarantee your remark will be
greeted with the most heartfelt reaction. And if you have
any questions about how to proceed, perhaps the following
conversation, overheard at a cocktail party, will shed some
light. It took place between a man who works as an associate producer for a TV station and a young woman to
whom he'd just been introduced by the host.

MAN: So, where do you know Bill from?
WOMAN: We went to college together.
MAN: Oh.
*Silence . . . with the woman looking about the room as if anxious
to meet other guests.*
MAN: Bill and I work for the same TV station.
WOMAN: That's nice.
MAN: I'm an associate producer in the news department.
WOMAN: I see.
Silence continues.
MAN: And what do you do?
WOMAN: I'm a space salesperson for a magazine.
MAN: Oh? That's funny. I was pretty sure you were some
    kind of model.
WOMAN: Me? A model? But I'm too short.
MAN: Well, I'm not an expert on what the requirements are,
    but you have that kind of modelly face.
WOMAN: What do you mean?
MAN: Oh, you know. Very fine features. Like you'd photo-
    graph well.
WOMAN: Really?
MAN: Like I said, I'm no expert, but you look like one of
    those women I see walking around town all the time with
    those big black modeling portfolios. I just assumed you
    were one of them.
WOMAN: Well, actually, I once did model a pair of flippers

for my Uncle Howard's sporting-goods store. But it was only for a dumb in-store poster.

MAN: Did you like it?

WOMAN: Yes, I did. It was fun.

MAN: Maybe you should do more of it.

WOMAN: I just never thought I had the height for it.

MAN: Well, you certainly have the face.

WOMAN: Thanks. Thanks a lot. That's very nice of you . . .

Of course with an approach like this you stand open to the accusation of being manipulative. But when you see the magic it works, the smiles, the giggling, the melting that occurs, you'll say, like me, so what's wrong with a little manipulation?

Gaze Deeply into Her Eyes

All right, you've got the ball rolling. You've asked her if she models, smiled a lot, established a conversational flow that doesn't feel as if it's going to dry up the moment you stop asking questions. In fact you're half beginning to think she may actually find you tolerable. Now it's time to turn the dial up a notch, to add a little intensity to this budding romance. How? By looking into her eyes when she talks to you—not casually, as if she's a Hertz girl asking whether you want collision insurance or not, but deeply, warmly, romantically. Really fixate on her irises. And try to pump as much passion into your own as possible.

I am not unmindful that this may require a bit of courage on your part. After all, gazing romantically into the depth of her soul is breathless stuff. It's hard not to blink or turn away or color with embarrassment.

Any discomfort you may feel, however, will be well worth it. Women like romance, mystery, intrigue. Most guys they meet are so pathetically ordinary and colorless. It excites women to finally run across a man who doesn't feel bound by convention to be plain, to be unadventurous. Let that be your guide across the whole spectrum of your dealings with women. The freer you feel around them to be different, to be romantic, to be impulsive, to make them feel that they are about to get involved with a man who is going to bring a little specialness and a little drama into their life, the more they will be attracted to you. So no matter how skittish it makes you feel, just bear down and look into her eyes, look so deeply you can see all the way down to her soul. It will make her dizzy. It will make you dizzy. It will make her tremble. It will make her wonder what it's like to be held in your arms.

Feel Your Sexuality

One of the most bizarre things that can happen to a man in the process of chatting with a girl he's been lusting after all night long from the far side of the room is that his lust suddenly disappears. This is not because upon closer examination the girl no longer appeals to him. Rather, it's because he's terrified—and as anyone who's ever been chased down the street by a ferocious Doberman knows, it's tough to feel horny when you're scared.

This can be a problem. When your natural sexuality is suppressed, it puts a damper on your entire personality, your sense of humor, your sense of passion, your drive to bring the relationship into a more personal arena.

This is not fatal, mind you. As I said before, there's a lot more room for dullness and silence in a relationship than you probably ever realized. On the other hand, it isn't great, either. First of all, who wants to be thought of as dull and sexless when he knows that deep down he's a hell of a guy. Second, after too long a dose of a boring man, even the politest of women can lose interest.

So here's something you can do about it: Feel your sexuality. No. I don't mean surreptitiously reach your hand into your pocket and . . . God knows, I don't mean that at all! What I am suggesting is that you find a way to rediscover your desire, your healthy animal attraction to the girl with whom you're trying to start a relationship.

How do you do that? Simple. Instead of listening to her drone on—she can be just as dull as you, you know—in answer to your question about the viability of a third major political party, let your eyes travel up and down her body. Look at her large, sensuous lips, or her full, round bosom, or her long, stately legs—whatever it was that drove you mad about her in the first place. Imagine the two of you alone on the sunbaked shore of a deserted island, naked, tan, breathless with desire. Try and feel all that mad, pent-up lust you carry around with you day and night but which mysteriously fled your body the moment you started talking with this tantalizing goddess. Imagine kissing her, drinking in the smell of her perfume, watching her step out of her skirt. Now there. See if that doesn't wake you up a bit, bring a little sparkle to your eye and a touch of color to your cheek. And now that you're feeling your old horny self again, don't hide it. Communicate it to her. With your fantasies about you and her playing in your mind, stare into her eyes. From the dreamy quality of your gaze she'll sense exactly what's there. And though it might frighten her a bit, it will arouse her even more. For certain, it won't bore her.

Believe me, I've tried this technique myself over the years, particularly when I've felt inadequate or not handsome, rich, or interesting enough. It's worked miracles. All of a sudden, instead of feeling sexless and shrinking and unworthy, you will start to feel your sense of potency and charisma come alive, no matter how intimidatingly beautiful the woman opposite you is.

Think of it this way. If the two of you really were trapped together on a deserted island, sooner or later you would take her to dizzying heights of sensual pleasure, even if at first she were not all that attracted to you. You are a male animal. You are physically capable of doing this. So why not tonight?

Touch Her

What, is he insane? Touch her. I hardly know her. She'll knee me in the groin, spray Mace in my eyes, call for the cops.

Calm down. I don't mean touch her bosom or her behind. Not yet anyway. I mean touch her arm or her shoulder, her hair, even her cheek. Remember, you're trying to break the bindings of formality and stiffness, trying to establish feelings of intimacy and attraction.

Little girls are always being touched by their fathers, having their hair rumpled, their hands held, their fannies tapped. Big girls still have a lot of little girl in them, and the yearning to be patted, massaged, and touched affectionately remains strong for life. So oblige them. Touch their arm and say, "What smooth skin." Or touch their hair and comment on its lovely color. Or touch their knee if you're seated side by side on a couch laughing over something funny that happened at the other end of the room. This is not to say, of course, that you should become grabby, laying your hands upon her every five seconds. Such an approach rapidly becomes annoying and its underlying motivation suspect. What you want to do is touch her when it seems appropriate, a natural part of the rhythm of your interaction.

Touching a woman sets up a bridge into her mind and her heart, a bridge over which feelings of attraction and warmth can pass back and forth. Not many guys have the guts to reach out and touch a girl's arm only minutes after first meeting. You may not have the guts, either. But if you can forge ahead and do it anyway, you'll be astonished at the results that ensue. Being a toucher says you're physical, sensuous, sexual. And it says it in a way that's perfectly dignified, acceptable, and easy for a girl to handle.

Let me tell you about a touching incident that happened to me when I was a twenty-year-old college student in New York City. The person who sat next to me in my Shakespeare course happened to be a married woman about twenty-five years old. She had the softest-looking blond hair I had ever seen, spun gold. One day, while the professor was droning on about some thane or other, she leaned over and whispered that it was her birthday. She smiled embarrassedly, as if it were somehow immodest to have volunteered that fact. I was so turned on by the shy look on her face I instinctively reached out and grazed the back of my hand across her cheek. Before I'd even begun to bring my hand back to my desk, I was getting ready to apologize. I hardly knew this woman. Plus she was married. Probably to a homicidally jealous hog butcher.

But you know what happened? The woman actually leaned into my touch, cooing softly as she did so. I could hardly believe it. Of course in those days I was far too much of a wimp to follow up with an invitation to coffee, a drink, an afternoon at the Gramercy Hotel. But it did teach me a lesson. One is perfectly free to reach out and touch nonprivate parts of a woman's body with damn near impunity. And in many cases it can yield surprisingly cordial results.

Talk Sexy

Over the years I have outraged countless people by recommending that men make sexy comments to women they hardly know. I didn't always think this was such a good idea. When I was a teenager, in fact, I used to think girls only liked men who were good. Upstanding. Fair. Polite. I would try to impress dates with my high ethical standards, my refusal to cheat on tests, my zeal in befriending nerds. I needn't tell you how infrequently I got laid. Then I witnessed an incident that was to be a major turning point in my life.

I was riding on a bus. In front of me sat a stunning young woman with long, lustrous black hair. At the next stop a man in chinos and a crew-neck sweater got on. He was interesting-looking, but not handsome. The instant he spotted the woman with the black hair, he made a beeline for her, passing several empty seats on the way. Sitting down next to her, he immediately started talking. For the most part it was idle chatter—what a slow bus, what a nice day. She answered him with what I perceived to be no more than minimal politeness. After a while, he asked what she did for a living. She replied she was the president of her own small research company.

"Oh, yeah," said the man, "do company presidents fuck?" I ducked down in my seat. Surely there was going to be an ugly scene, the culmination of which would most likely be the burly bus driver's throwing the young man off the bus. But the melee I was expecting did not occur. Slowly, cautiously, I sat back up in my seat. The woman was staring at the man with grim fascination. "Yes," she said quietly. They exited the bus together.

Now I don't hold this example up as something that happens every day (although I'm not sure that it doesn't). Nor do I suggest you attempt such a bold and blatant approach yourself. You are much more likely to be arrested than invited home to bed.

No, the reason I cite the above case is that for me it was so apocalyptic, so mind-opening. All of a sudden, in one fell swoop, it made me realize that one of my major assumptions about the opposite sex was all wrong. Women are not titillated by exalted behavior any more than men are. Their fantasies aren't piqued, nor their id provoked, by goody-goodies, clergymen, celibates, and moral leaders. Oh, they may admire them, but they don't have sexual fantasies about them. What does turn them on is much more closely related to what turns us on—drinking wine, nude bathing in the moonlight, sexy movies, and the like.

From there on in, I began to notice that men who do well with women tend to be much more open and sexual in the things they say to them than I had ever realized: "You have a terrific figure," "bedroom eyes," "a fantastic ass," "incredible breasts," and this often only minutes after first meeting them.

Naturally, you can't say something sexy during the first five minutes of conversation to every woman you meet. Some will spit in your eye. Some will gasp in horror. You have to use your antennae. You have to make an educated guess as to who will respond positively and who will think you're a pervert. But when in doubt, I say go ahead and throw caution to the wind. The worst that can happen is a slap in the face. And the best that can happen—and it'll happen a whole lot more frequently than you'd imagine—is that you and the girl will shortly thereafter become lovers. Talking sexy is that powerful! These days almost as many women are into one-night stands as men (stands to reason mathematically). And when you let them know what a sexually oriented guy you are, they'll instantly realize you're their kind of man.

Exactly *how* do you talk sexy to a woman? Tell her she has a fantastic figure and is giving you unprintable sex fantasies. Declare that if you could only see her naked you would be quite willing to die, your life's dream fulfilled beyond all expectations. Remark upon her unparalleled behind, her sensuous hips, her lips that are making you thirsty for her kisses. If you can, try to say all this with a bit of a smile, as if you're only half serious. It'll make it that much easier for her to listen without having to fear that she's giving you tacit permission to take her to bed.

Yes, a few uptight women will pretend to be annoyed. But most healthy, outgoing, life-loving women will be flattered and in many cases turned on. Beneath our highly socialized, civilized exteriors, we are all still animals, she as well as you. Don't ever forget it. The man who knows this—not just intellectually but in his bones, his cells, and his blood—will never have trouble succeeding with women.

Above all, on our most basic biological level, men are sex objects to women and women are sex objects to men. That is what spurs procreation, ensures our survival as a species. And don't let anyone ever tell you different. People may not *want* life to work that way. But that cannot alter the fact that life *does* work that way.

Be Extravagant

Just as a lot of men feel it's cool to scowl and to spit out tough-sounding monosyllables, there are others who think it's de rigueur to be suspicious, hard, stingy. Oh, they may feel an impulse to buy a girl a drink, but a moment later comes the counter impulse: She's using me.

Let me give you a bit of advice. Stop worrying about being used. Women are turned on by generosity and extravagance. For every one woman who attempts to "use" you, there will be a dozen who are joyously, deliriously, lovingly moved by your magnanimous nature. I know it's corny, but watch what happens when you instruct your waiter to deliver a champagne cocktail to the pretty blonde across the room. She'll smile, blush, giggle, and keep on turning to look at the mysterious, bighearted stranger who had the style and good taste to send over genuine bubbly! Wow!

If you're rich, of course, it's easy to be extravagant. But even if you're not, the few extra dollars it takes to be a sport is often well worth the investment. For example, let's say you've met a woman in a noisy singles bar. The drinks in here may only be a dollar fifty, but maybe it's an impossible place to talk, to weave your magic, to get well beyond your opening line. Why not suggest the two of you hop in a cab and go to the poshest bar in town? Chances are she's heard of the place but has never been there before.

Imagine the impression you'll make by being the first one to take her there. It'll tell her a whole multitude of good things about you: You're not afraid to spend your money; you think she's special enough to bring to the Oak Room, Polo Lounge, Ritz Carlton bar, or wherever the hell it is you're going; you've got taste; you're going places.

Drinks in the fanciest place around are rarely more than a dollar higher than in the seediest joint in the worst section of town. So why not go for it?

Here are a few other ways to be expansive. Buy her a corsage from the flower lady canvassing the bar. Throw down your dip-coated carrot stick in disgust and say, "Yuck! Let's go out and get a decent meal." And do it. Take her to a good French restaurant.

Or rent yourself a limousine for the evening as you cruise the various singles bars and discos. It'll cost you about a hundred bucks. Big deal. Of course, as your driver deposits you and her in front of her apartment for the night, don't pretend he'll be there in the morning. Let your new friend know the truth, that you were just in the mood to indulge yourself. That's impressive enough.

So loosen up, guys. Stop squirreling away all your grimy little greenbacks. Inflation is eroding the life out of them. Might as well put them to use in a good cause. And I'd like to know a better cause than winning the woman of your dreams.

Be Nuts

I wish I could give insanity lessons. Ninety percent of the guys I meet seem like they're busting their butts trying to be saner and more normal to fit in better with the crowd. They wear the right after-shave and the correct jeans; they see the in movies. What a waste of time! Women like madmen. Now by that I don't mean rapists, catatonics, and advanced schizophrenics. What I mean by *madmen* is oddballs, mavericks, rebels, men who follow their own muse instead of everybody else's. Boy, if you're not afraid to do that, you'll not only get beyond the opening line, you'll get beyond her front door, her bedroom door, and just about any other barrier you might find in your way.

So if you have a tendency to be a little off-the-wall, don't try to curb it. Think of it this way. She may have a dull job in a dull company, no boyfriends, dull girlfriends, dull parents, and live on a dull street. Most of life is like that, you know. Chances are hers is, too.

Remember, there is a tremendous inertia to life. It's basic, it's bedrock. That's why society has such a need for its Bill Murrays, Dan Akroyds, Robin Williamses, and Steve Martins. None of these guys is that classically good-looking, but, oh, do they attract women. Why? Because they make a girl feel alive, make her feel the potential life has for excitement, kicks, drama. I'm not saying you should try to act like a lunatic if it's not really in you. But if you are an offbeat, bohemian, eccentric, freaky fellow, for God's sake don't hide it from the ladies. It's probably the most magnetic trait you have going for you.

10

How to Move On

The other day I was doing a radio interview on the subject of my first book, *How to Pick Up Girls,* when a listener called in with an anecdote he thought I'd like. It seems that several months ago the caller had stopped in at a local discotheque. After standing around for a few minutes, he'd spotted a group of women sitting at a table in the rear. One of them caught his fancy. He marched up and in earshot of the lady's four gawking girlfriends said, "Would you like to dance?"

"Hah!" she snorted contemptuously. "Not with you." Her friends all tittered.

"That's okay," he retorted. "I had to go to the bathroom anyway." And with that he turned and walked away.

Less than half an hour later, while he was sitting at the bar nursing a lonely beer, the woman who had just shot him down walked up. "I like your style," she confessed coquettishly. The caller allowed that he and his new friend went on to spend one of the greatest evenings of his life.

The moral? If you do happen to get rejected while pursuing a woman, there's no need to go to pieces. You're even allowed to fight back. Sometimes your very anger will turn a woman on, show her you're not a man to be pushed around. I have an acquaintance who, whenever a woman refuses to dance with him, responds in all innocence, "Then I suppose sex is out of the question?" He's been wrong a surprising number of times.

Circulate

I have a friend who commissions scripts for a big television producer. He says he often looks at two hundred ideas before giving a writer the go-ahead.

A man I play tennis with buys multifamily real estate developments. He usually has to look at over twenty-five properties before he finds one that appeals to him.

What does this have to do with getting beyond the opening line? If you're having a rough go of it with one particular woman—she's unresponsive, suicidal, headed for a nunnery—move on. Cut bait. Find someone else.

You can't appeal to every woman you approach. And not every woman you approach will wind up appealing to you. So don't turn a five-minute introductory conversation into a strained, forced, full-evening's chore. It's no disgrace to call it quits and excuse yourself. In fact, better you beat her to the punch. Just mosey on to the next woman who catches your eye. And if that doesn't work, move on again.

Random attraction is one of the mysteries of life. Just when you're sure there's not a woman in the entire world who's going to be turned on by you, you'll find a dozen, maybe more.

So keep circulating. Not every girl can like you. But, oh brother, how sweet it is when you meet the one who does.

Look at All the Girls

While you're circulating, consider this. It's important to look at *all* the women, not just the ones who resemble Cheryl Tiegs. It is easy to fall into the trap of pursuing only those women who society tells us are attractive and pass right on by those who, on the surface anyway, don't seem all that good-looking.

This is a mistake. There are easily five times as many women as you think with whom you could fall in love. So the next time you wander through a party, muttering to yourself that there's no one good here, stop. Concentrate. Take a second glance. Force yourself to look beyond her frizzy hair, her too plump arms, her corny horn-rimmed glasses. Take in her breasts, her backside, the color of her eyes, the sound of her voice, her facial structure. Let her gestalt flood across the surface of your mind, your body. See if you feel any spark. I'll bet you do—in fact, far more frequently and intensely than you ever expected to. And I'll tell you why. The smoldering sexuality and passion of a woman who has been overlooked because she does not have obvious prettiness is just dying to be released and is ready to come alive. And when it does, watch out. If you can handle it, you're in for the evening, the weekend, the season of your life.

Insisting on a standardly pretty girl is narcissistic, a signal to the outside world that you're capable of landing a sought-after prize. It often has little to do with the quality of your sexual and emotional union with her. Conversely, you may have the most exquisite sex, the most soaring good times with a woman at whom most men wouldn't stop to look twice. So what? You're not dating girls to please the guys. You're doing it for yourself. So next time you're at a party and all the other guys in the room are tripping over each other vying for a smile from the same dame, give a long, hard look at all the other girls in the room. I'm sure that you'll find at least one who, upon closer examination, moves you more than you anticipated. Try some of the aforementioned ploys on her. I hope you have a lot of stamina. You're going to have the night of your life. And watch how pretty she looks in the morning. Sometimes all that a less glamorous woman needs to bring out her beauty is a man who knows how to touch her, talk to her, love her.

11

The Basics

In the preceding chapters we explored where to meet women, how to break the ice with them, and then how to keep the ball rolling long enough to collect a telephone number or make a date to see one another again. In this chapter, perhaps the most critical in the book, I'm going to assume that you have just begun dating a woman (or several women) and want to make sure that your new relationship turns out to be every bit as fulfilling, both from an emotional and sexual standpoint, as you want it to be. The following are several basic strategies to try to adhere to throughout your relationship.

Be Considerate

Last year I hosted a television show in Columbus, Ohio. I do a lot of television shows, but this one was made special because it was on a unique cable system that allows viewers to respond to questions by pressing buttons on their sets.

This is a great device, and I was naturally eager to put it to use. One of the questions I addressed to the women in the audience was: "What attracts you to a man most? (a) Looks; (b) Dress; (c) Consideration; or (d) Money/Good Job?"

Consideration won hands down with a whopping forty-six percent. The runner-up was looks, but at twenty-one percent it was not even half as popular. And the others trailed even further behind.

The response did not really surprise me. For years I've been touting the importance of showing women consideration. I was happy, though, to see my contention so thoroughly corroborated.

Consideration as a theme runs through most of this book as well. How could I avoid it? It is the essence of how to succeed with women—in all stages and aspects of a relationship. From meeting a woman to marrying her, from the dance floor to the bedroom, being considerate is the one necessary constant. Never let it slip too far from your center of awareness.

Consideration is easy. All you have to do is ask yourself: *What does she want? What would be good for her? What can I do to make her day more pleasant?* More than any of the particular gestures you make, it is this supportive attitude that women respond to. It presses the right button.

The Importance of Humor

We live in a world that takes itself far too seriously. This is especially the case when it comes to male-female relations. People act so uptight and serious. You'd think someone was dying.

If you can break out of the serious mode of relating to the opposite sex, you've got a step up on ninety-five percent of the competition. Most guys seem to forget that it takes a smile to turn women on. They ask for a date as if they're proposing a corporate merger or something equally as sterile and businesslike. And when they ask a woman to go to bed with them, their countenance makes it seem as if they've just been told they have cancer.

But the message that should be got across is "Hey, let's have a good time together. Let's blow off our troubles and cares and get loose." And this is a message that can only be communicated with a smile.

The next stage of good humor is laughing. Laughter relaxes women, soothes women, and at the same time turns women on. It is your great ally in the march toward intimacy. So find reasons to promote laughter when you're with women. Tell a good joke. Tell a bad joke. Do an impersonation of Ronald Reagan. Do one of your old high-school biology teacher. What you do doesn't matter, at least up to a point. The important thing is to have a good time doing it.

One of the best pickups I ever witnessed—unfortunately, I did not participate in this one—took place at a baseball game. An almost goofy-looking kid with glasses walked right up to a beautiful blonde about nineteen years of age—really just a scrumptious-looking girl—pointed to her, and exclaimed, "Ugly! Ugly!" She burst into laughter. Apparently no one had ever said that to her before.

"You're so ugly," the boy went on, "I better buy you a beer. No one else will." And he did so, sitting down next to her; she seemed to like that, for they talked and laughed throughout the entire game.

The kid's style was so off-the-wall it made me realize something. Anything can be funny as long as you yourself think it is. And as long as your humor is sure not to hurt anybody's feelings. The girl in the above anecdote was, for instance, so attractive that there was absolutely no chance of her taking seriously the comment that she was ugly. With a lesser creature there might indeed be some ambiguity. So with that kind of humor especially, be careful. Don't tread on anybody's feet.

In other chapters I talk about different items or techniques that work as aphrodisiacs. There is no more important one than humor. Often it will do far more to aid your cause than wine, money, or good looks.

Be Romantic

The importance of romance, as with humor, cannot be overstated. All women seek it in their lives, and the man who understands this holds the key to success with them. He will always have an edge on other men.

Being romantic is the difference between being an adolescent and being an adult in the world of love. Put romance in your relationships with women and you will never be thought of again as simply another guy. You will have the look, the air, the stride of a lover. You will be the kind of man that all women seek.

What is it about romance that is so important to women? "For me romance is the difference between merely existing and living life to the fullest," says Vicki, a slender brunette who works for a prestigious art gallery on Manhattan's upper East Side. "If it weren't for the possibility of getting some in my life, I wouldn't even bother to go out with men. That's how important it is."

Vicki is not alone. All women thrive on romance, but they are almost universally frustrated by its absence from the world today. Many would gladly give up washing machines, dishwashers, and the other conveniences of modern life if they could only get a little bit of romance back in their lives. But men won't cooperate.

"Nothing annoys me more," added Darlene, one of Vicki's co-workers, "than the fact that most men don't even bother to be the slightest bit romantic. It takes so little effort."

As I explained to Darlene, the reason that men are not very romantic today is not because they won't put in the effort, but because they're not sure what being romantic means. They're afraid of coming off as just corny, old-fashioned, or foolish.

The best way I can help men get over this problem is by giving a proper definition of romance. It does not entail feigning a foreign accent, or only drinking imported wines, or changing your name from Joe to Pierre. There is absolutely no pretension involved. What it does entail is going out of your way—if only a little bit—to make a woman feel special and to make the time you spend together seem special as well.

How can you do this? Easy. All that a woman requires to feel special is to know that you think and care about her. Sending cards, flowers, and small gifts is a simple and inexpensive way to achieve this. You need not send a dozen roses. Often a simple carnation will do.

As for the time you spend together, you need not be a magician to achieve magical results. The first rule is to be especially courteous, by opening doors, seating her, and so on. Make the dinners you have together intimate, candle-lit affairs. And if you're at your place together, little gestures, like disconnecting your phone and playing soft music, will give her the feeling of having entered a special world. Increase this feeling by making sure that all her needs are met.

Most women will tell you that their most romantic experiences have been spontaneous ones—a walk along the beach at night holding hands, an impromptu drive into the country for a picnic, a bottle of wine shared in front of a fireplace on a cold winter night. These are some activities that you can't always plan out. But by merely putting yourself in a romantic frame of mind, you make it inevitable that this type of experience will come your way.

The greatest advantage to being romantic is that it puts you and the woman you're with in your own private union. It evokes an us-against-the-world type of feeling. In her mind there will be no room for other men. Instead she will feel only the irresistible sensation of being drawn closer and closer to your warmth, gentleness, and protectiveness. As she basks in the warm, romantic glow you emanate, the mundane and petty world will seem far, far away. No woman could ask for any more.

Be Unique

How can you stand out among your fellow men? How do you make yourself seem like the special man that a woman decides is the type she should definitely become involved with?

The solution is far simpler than you might think. There is no hocus-pocus to perform, nor any radical altering of your appearance or personality. Rather, it entails emphasizing certain aspects of yourself that are naturally appealing to women. This can be done through basic techniques that most men tend to ignore or overlook, perhaps because they are looking for more complex or magical procedures. But once you become aware of what you should do, it will seem laughingly simple to make yourself uniquely appealing to women.

"All the world is a stage," the Great Bard said, and the best actors get the biggest parts, I will add. So when you're out in public, *act* like the kind of guy women take notice of, the guy who maximizes his opportunities to be courteous.

If public displays of chivalry seem a little funny to you, do them with a smile on your face. In this day and age it may not be the norm, but who said you should try to be normal? After all, what you're after is *standing out*. And the important thing is that opening doors, offering your seat on the bus, that whole bit can score you a lot of points with the opposite sex. It turns women on and is particularly impressive with dates. In fact, when you see the results you get, your acts of courtesy will probably become more and more theatrical. Don't hold back.

If you're in a restaurant that you don't like, don't hide your discontent. Tell your date that you know a better place. She'll be impressed that you don't put up with what you don't like. Conversely, if you're enjoying a film that you're seeing together, let her know. It will increase her enjoyment of the film.

The point is that it's good to let a woman know that you don't just passively interact with your environment. You respond to it.

"Guys who don't speak their mind are a drag to be with," Cheryl, an airline stewardess, told me. "I'd rather spend time with someone who was a little bit on the obnoxious side than a guy who acted like a complete zombie. At least I'd feel there was some communication."

Cheryl's attitude is representative of most women's— almost any response is better than none. Your opinions are important because they are your opinions. Don't be afraid to let them out.

There is one important qualification to all this, however, that you should always keep in mind. Don't make "you" the subject of all your opinions. Women do not want to hear— and men don't either, for that matter—a long spiel on your own greatness. Even an inadvertently self-aggrandizing remark can gum up a conversation. So even if you did win the Nobel Prize, let her find out about it on the news. This kind of impressive information about you will come out sooner or later anyway.

The other side of this coin, practiced by a smaller percentage of men but just as blunderous a conversational technique, is masochistic self-dissection. Being humble is one thing; being verbally self-abusive is another altogether. Certainly self-honesty is an important feature of a decent relationship, but hard-core self-revelations shouldn't be sprung on somebody before they've got a chance to know you. So don't let out all your fears, insecurities, doubts, and misgivings over your first dinner date together. Because when you tell a woman that you feel like nobody, that's pretty much the opinion she's going to have of you, too. And who knows? Left to make her own observations, her opinion of you may be a good deal more flattering than your own.

Have you ever said to a woman you're not involved with, "Wow, are you sexy!" Or, "You're the woman of my dreams!" Or even just, "I'd like to get to know you better." If you haven't been so bold, you've been missing out on one of the surefire ways there is to distinguish yourself from the rest of the scenery.

Sure, some uptight women may be a little put out, but most ladies will enjoy it if you show a sense of humor, if you don't leer, drool, or pant as you make your remark, if you act like a nice guy. *Women notice the man who notices them.*

I heard the following from Suzy, a stunning, raven-haired West Coast model, who told me that the best thing about her relationship with her boyfriend Dave is the way he always manages to give mystique to their get-togethers.

"Dave and I never meet at each other's place. No, that would be too ordinary. He always comes up with the craziest places to rendezvous, and hardly ever the same one twice. A public fountain, in a costume shop, even in a coed sauna—we've met all over the place. One time David met me at the beach, which would be ordinary enough, but he was *naked!* I should add that it was at night. We ended up making love right there."

Meeting a girl at an unusual spot may not always lead to impromptu lovemaking, but it can't help but push you in that direction. It's that first dash of spice in whatever plans you're cooking up for each other, an early injection of intrigue and romance, that will take effect even before you've laid eyes on one another.

Kids know naturally how to have fun, and most of us

could stand to learn a few lessons from them. Why do we become so obsessed with seeming serious, sober, respectable—especially while we're courting someone—when we get older? In my opinion that's a step in the wrong direction.

What most men need to do is loosen up, learn to be more like a ten-year-old. Have you ever noticed how grown women can't seem to keep their hands off little boys? And most women would like to get more fun out of the time they spend with men than they usually do.

So on your next date, race her to the car, or make a snowman together, or just sing a song. Don't worry, you won't be laughed at. Women tend to be much less repressed about childlike frolicking than men are. And the little girl in a woman is a delightful creature to get to know.

Never settle for a conventional, ho-hum interaction or get-together. There's always a way to put some excitement into time spent together. It might entail going roller-skating late at night or taking a long walk all bundled up during a snowstorm. It might be in the form of a joint before going to see a movie or champagne on your lunch break. Don't be pushy about these things, just enthusiastic. Because it's ultimately a spirit of enthusiasm that will distinguish you from the masses.

One of the characteristics that women most look for in men is uniqueness—the courage and the capacity to be a little bit atypical.

Unfortunately, far too many guys think that the way to score with women is to be more typical, to fit in better with the crowd. This works up to a point, but wearing the same clothes as everybody else, going to the same places, and saying the same lines will only take you so far and, what's worse, will drop you right there. If you're attracted to exciting and original women, you should be that way too; and the only way you can do this is by abandoning the life preserver of conformity. Then you really can start swimming. Your stroke? Freestyle, of course.

A Little Patience

Some guys get married at eighteen, either because they're berserkly in love or because they've got a girlfriend who is putting pressure on them, and they're terrified that if they ever let her go they'll never find anyone else.

Have patience, my friend, have patience. If you're presently going with a woman you're not all that crazy about, and she's bugging you to make it for keeps, perhaps you should tell her you're not ready yet. Once, when I was in my early twenties and shooting an ad with the great fashion photographer Richard Avedon, I happened to mention that I was contemplating getting married in a few months. The man pulled his eye away from the lens, turned to me with the grimmest of expressions, and implored me to wait until I was older, until I'd established myself, until I had some money in the bank. Otherwise, he implied, I'd attract a far less attractive woman than I deserved and would be miserable for the rest of my days. I was stunned by the passion of his plea, for the man hardly knew me. I had the feeling that he was speaking from his own experience, that he had married very young out of insecurity and *then* got rich and famous. (Happily, by the way, I did not take his advice. I was marrying Joanna because I *wanted* to.)

The moral here, of course, is that a man with experience and position and possessions can attract more women and superior women than a twenty-one-year-old kid without a penny to his name, even one who looks and dances like John Travolta. So if you're a guy who is confident he's going somewhere, maybe it would be wise for you to wait until you get there before you hook up with a lady for life. I realize this sounds a trifle cold and calculating, but so be it. If you want to attract a truly stunning woman, this may be one of the strategies you have to resort to. I've known many a hard-driving, talented young guy who devoted his early years to working his butt off until he could afford to buy his own service station or liquor store or was made manager of his office and *then*—when he was driving the car he wanted, living in a great apartment, wearing better clothes—went out and won himself the kind of woman he'd always dreamed about. Maybe you're a guy who just knows that you're destined to make it big one day. Maybe you should be a little patient yourself.

A Little Rethinking

When we look in the mirror, many of us home right in on the very thing we like least about our appearance—a nose like a banana, eyes set too close together, giant ears, tiny mouth, pimple patch around the chin. And then we head out to a bar or a party or a dance with an image printed indelibly across our mind of ourself as Nose or Ear or Pimple or Bald Spot and assume that that is exactly how we appear to others.

Know something? How you see yourself often has almost nothing to do with how others perceive you. When people look at you, they see you as a blending of your features, your good ones as well as your bad ones. Often, others will actually idealize your appearance, concentrating on the good and trying to ignore the bad, just as you do when a blind date opens the door and you can't decide whether she's pretty or not. You want her to be great, of course, and so your mind and eyes do everything they can to give her the benefit of the doubt.

Remember this the next time you walk up to a girl in a singles bar, ducking your head and averting your eyes, sure that she's not going to like what she sees. The truth is, she's on your side, wanting to like you simply because you've

approached her; and she's exaggerating your attractiveness, just as you would be doing if she came up to you.

Women aren't as narrow-minded about looks as men are.
So even if you're not in love with your own looks, don't
assume others won't be. I have a friend who bumped into a
girl from his chemistry lab on the way to class one day. She
was a ravishing blonde with eyes as green as emeralds. She
and my friend had a passing relationship, and so she fell in
step beside him as they walked across campus. Secretly my
pal cursed his luck, for he had been up all night cramming
for a big test and felt he looked like a junkie, his eyes red,
their sockets hollow and dark. Plus his complexion, not
good to begin with, was in one of its more eruptive states.
Damn, he found himself thinking, *why couldn't I have run into
her at a dance or at the Rat, when I'd just washed my hair and had a
chance to shave.* And so when the girl volunteered out of the
blue, "You know, Dan, my friends and I think you're one of
the cutest guys in chem lab," he thought he was hearing
things. Astonishing! Dan had thought himself one of the
ugliest.

The reason I think it's so important for you to realize that
you are far from the best judge of your own looks is that it
may help you to keep going at those times when you most
want to hide in a closet. Hair not lying just right? So what!
Get out to that dance or party anyway. You never can tell
when a magnificent woman is going to find *you* pretty magnificent, too.

We've all heard the story about the short, pudgy, crude
guy who walks away with the beautiful girl who's been
sitting alone at the bar all evening long because all the
other guys have been too afraid of rejection to approach
her. Know *why* we've all heard it? Because it's happened so
many times it's become a legend.

The interpretation, of course, is that the short, funny-
looking guy wins the girl because he's the only one who
asks. But I think there's another factor at play. I think a

woman is somewhat awed by a man who has the courage to approach her when all the other men she sees are just standing around, seemingly too paralyzed with fear to step forward. It tells her a whole host of good things about the one who did, whether he's good-looking or not, things that communicate on a most fundamental, biological level. Perhaps he'll make a most worthy mate . . . one who goes after what he wants in business, in taking care of his family, in making sure his woman and children will have the best that life can give them.

Never forget that most women still feel more secure, protected, and loved around a man who is willing to take charge than around one who is sending out vibes that he's ashamed of the way he looks and talks (or one who is handsome and little else). And therefore the very act of approaching an attractive woman will make you handsomer in her eyes. Think about that next time you're lurking in the corner with all the other guys, wishing you were so good-looking girls would come on to you. That's not what a woman wants from you. She wants you to get up the guts, no matter how scared you feel, and walk over and say hello. That alone will make you look like Paul Newman in her eyes, more than all the pretty boys in the place.

12

How to Win Dates with Hard-to-Get Women

Has this ever happened to you? A girl comes to work in your office, or starts sitting next to you in calculus class, or moves into the apartment right down the hall. There's nothing particularly unusual about the arrival of someone new in your daily routine except that this girl happens to be spectacular. Whatever it is about women that drives you berserk—heart-shaped lips, platinum hair, a voice like Stevie Nicks's, a bust like Lady Diana's—she's got it in spades. Your mind is starting to swell with dizzying images of the two of you glued together on a beach in Ibiza, which in case you don't know is an island in the Mediterranean that has been described as the most erotic strip of land in the entire world. And so, despite the fact that you're convinced that maybe this girl is a bit too delicious-looking for the likes of you, you decide you'd kind of like to take her out to a movie or dinner one night before some more assertive chap tucks her under his arm and carries her off into the sunset.

So you scout around, find out her telephone number, and scribble it on a piece of paper, which you carry around in your pocket for a couple of weeks trying to get up the nerve to call. The inspiration comes one night while you're sitting in front of "Little House on the Prairie."

Suddenly it hits you that you're spending more time gazing into Michael Landon's eyes than the eyes of the girl of your dreams. So you yank her telephone number out of your pocket and, with trembling forefinger, dial. As the phone rings, you are surprised to find that at least part of you is hoping she's not at home. No such luck.

"Hello," she answers in a voice that sounds every bit as suspicious and aloof as that of your grammar-school principal, old Miss Volnay.

"Uh, hi. Is this Saundra?"

"This is she."

"The Saundra with red hair who works in research?"

"Who is this?"

"Um, this is Joe."

"Joe who?"

"Uh, Joe, the guy from over in shipping."

"I'm afraid I don't know you."

"Yeah, you know, the guy with lightish brown hair who sits next to Marion Hazleton, the heavyish woman with the mole on her cheek. You and I once talked about what a rainy day it was on the coffee line."

"Oh, yes. I think I remember now." *Thinks* she remembers!

"Um, well, what I wanted to know, Saundra, is that maybe if you're not doing anything this Friday night you might want to come to the movies with me. There's a James Dean revival at the Cinematheque. They're showing *East of Eden.*"

"I'm sorry. I'm busy Friday."

"Oh, okay. Maybe some other time," you mumble and hang up the phone, convinced that it was sheer folly of you to so much as *dream* of a date with someone as sublime as the lissome Saundra. To have actually gone ahead and called her was utter madness. As you resume your seat in front of the tube, you vow never again to attempt to reach so far over your head. You resign yourself to spending the rest of your days with women who are okay but don't really drive you mad.

Well, you don't think I'm going to leave you stranded here do you? The jacket copy on this book promises to show you how to win a date with a woman who at first seems cold to your advances. And that's exactly what I intend to do. I know that at times it may seem impossible to succeed in warming up a girl who acts as if she's got ice water running through her arteries. Indeed, sometimes it is impossible. On the other hand, the situation is often far more promising than most men realize. Of course, to bring this promise to life one needs a plan. And I'm fairly confident that you'll find the following four-point system unusually effective. It's been developed over a period of about ten years with a lot of bumps and scrapes and hurt feelings. But just about all the hitches are out of it now, and I think you'll find that it's going to help you win the companionship and even the love of a lot of women who at first seemed as if they wanted to have nothing to do with you.

Be Magnanimous

Every time I pick up the paper these days I come across an article that says that our national vocabulary is shrinking. So let me give you the definition of *magnanimous* found in the great Random House Dictionary of the English Language: "Generous in forgiving an insult or injury; free from petty resentfulness or vindictiveness."

There's no other way to define step one of our program. *Be magnanimous.* Be generous in forgiving poor Saundra for not having been free to go out with you. Avoid sounding petty or resentful, even if deep down inside—or not so deep down inside—you're sore as hell.

For example, if she replies, "I'm sorry, but I'm busy Friday," don't let your voice betray your hurt, your humiliation, your suspicion that she's not really busy. Instead, declare, "Oh, that's perfectly all right. I'll call you next week. You really look like someone I'd like to know better." Be complimentary, cheerful, upbeat, and positive.

But won't that make me seem like some kind of gullible rube?

To the contrary, it will make you sound confident and urbane and sophisticated. Saundra, or whoever, will think to herself, *Hey, this guy is different. Instead of going to pieces and sounding like a hurt little boy who didn't get whatever he was hoping to get for Christmas, he sounds mature, able to handle disappointment, confident in his attractiveness to women.*

To be magnanimous will wake a woman up about you. She'll wonder if perhaps she didn't make a mistake in rejecting you so fast. When she shows up at work or school the next day, she'll be on the lookout for you, curious to see if you still seem as unruffled and friendly toward her. So be sure when you see her in the hall or at the watercooler that you are. Continue to *be magnanimous.* Tell her, "Gee, I was really sorry you couldn't make it to the movies with me. I think it would have been a lot of fun. Oh, well, I'll call you again soon."

And keep it up, every chance you get. Be friendly, be open, be generous-spirited. She'll start to see you as a man who really values himself (even if secretly you're sometimes not all that high on yourself). After all, who else could continue to be so amiable toward her but a man who had no doubts that she really was busy?

Be Persistent

Over the past few months a lot of men who take my course "How to Meet Women" have asked if it pays to be persistent in pursuing a woman who doesn't seem all that anxious to be pursued. They pose the question in a way that leads me to believe they want me to say, "No, forget her. Move on to someone else."

Sorry guys, I can't let you off the hook that easily. For the reality is, it very much pays to be persistent. I recall hearing Patricia Neal say on a talk show that her then husband, the writer Roald Dahl, had called her approximately thirty times in a row before she finally acceded to his request for a lunch date. Shortly after, they were married.

I have a friend who followed a lovely willowy blonde through Greenwich Village one summer evening, trying to get her into conversation. After ten minutes of brutal silence she finally responded, *"Je ne parle pas anglais* [I don't speak English]."

"Ô, mais je parle français [I speak French]," responded my pal. They stopped at a bar, had drinks, and then went back to her apartment, capping an evening that he relishes to this day.

A few paragraphs back I recommended that you magnanimously tell a woman, "I'll call you next week." That wasn't just there to take up space. Do call her next week. And be just as magnanimous, even if she still happens to be busy. And call her next week and the following week, all the while keeping up your cheerful, friendly, generous-spirited front. The chances are excellent that she'll soon accept a date with you, either to get you off her back (in which case you'll have a chance to charm her in person) or because she's started to think, *Hmm, this guy is really brimming with confidence and belief in himself. Maybe there's more to him than I thought.* You

have no idea how this can turn a woman's mind around
about you.

Be Disarming

Okay, let's say you've called a woman half a dozen times
without success. You've been unfailingly magnanimous and
obviously persistent. But still you've got nowhere. Now
what do you do?

Step 3 in our plan to win a date with a distant, aloof
woman is to confront her. You must still continue to be
pleasant and friendly, never bitter-sounding or petty, but
now is the time to ask her why she seems so dead set in her
resolve not to go out with you. How do you do that? Witness the following conversation.

SHE: I'm sorry, Joe, but I'm busy this Friday.

YOU: Ah, what a shame. I was really looking forward to
going out with you. Why don't we make it next Friday,
then?

SHE: I'm busy then, too.

YOU: Boy, I'm really running into a streak of bad luck here.
Are these dates all with one guy?

SHE: Uh, not really.

YOU: Well then, what am I doing wrong, Saundra? I'm not
asking you to marry me, you know. I just thought it would
be fun to catch a movie together.

SHE: I'm sorry, Joe, but I'm just not attracted to you.

YOU: So? Who says you have to be so attracted to me? All
I'm suggesting is that we spend two hours in front of a
movie screen together, maybe have a glass of wine afterward. What do you say? If you can't make it Friday, how
about an off night? How does next Wednesday look?

SHE: Gee, I don't know . . .

YOU: Oh, come on. How's it going to hurt? I'm a nice,

friendly guy, clean, generous, a good listener. Besides, I grow on people.

SHE: Well . . .

YOU: Hey, terrific. I'll pick you up at eight.

SHE: Well, all right. But, remember, I've got to be home early.

YOU: Me, too. I've got to get my beauty sleep, so you'll be more attracted to me. See you at eight.

Now I'm sure that some of you guys out there are thinking, *Sure, sure, of course it works in a book. It's rigged.*

Well, let me tell you something. I've seen the above technique used on dozens of occasions, and it's worked on at least half of them. You'd be astonished at how flattering it is for a woman to be pursued with such zeal. And at how unique she finds the man who's got courage enough to call her on her coldness. And when a woman feels flattered, she can't help but start to feel warm and affectionate to the guy who's flattering her.

Believe me, people don't want to be cold to others. It's a strain. It makes them feel guilty. This woman who's been resisting your charms? She may not be immune to them, but by having started out on a cold tack she may not know how to gracefully go about reversing herself. So help her out. Ask her as directly and politely as you can why she's not accepting your request to spend a few hours with her. You may very well find that she's suddenly decided to change her mind.

Ask Her to Lunch

Earlier we discussed the importance of consideration. It's more than holding the door open for a woman and lighting her cigarette. These are just symbols of consideration, signs that show her you're more than attracted to her —you *like* and *respect* her. Here's another symbol of consideration: Ask her out to lunch before you ask her to spend an entire evening with you.

Why is this being considerate? Because it takes into account the many conflicting feelings she may have about you. *Yes, I like him, but I don't know him yet.* Or, *I think I'd like to date him, but I keep weekend nights for my steady boyfriend.*

In short, when you make your first date with a woman a date for lunch, it says to her: (a) you're not going to make a heavy sexual pass at her; (b) you're aware that she may be having doubts about what you're really like; and, (c) you like her enough to be willing to let her grow to like you at her speed, not yours.

The lunch date is also a particularly good way of getting together with a woman you're a little bit nervous about asking out, one you're not sure wants to go out with you. Nothing seems more casual than a proposal to get together for lunch. Where ordinarily a woman might put up some resistance, with a lunch date that impulse will be stymied. She'll think to herself, *Oh sure, it's only for lunch. Why not?* Meanwhile you get a great opportunity to let your charms loose on her.

For any woman you meet who works near you, lunch may well be the most convenient time to get together. A five- or ten-minute walk can bring you into contact not only with each other but with dozens, if not hundreds, of restaurants to choose from. Indeed in some downtown areas the variety may well exceed that which is available at night.

And what could be easier to ask for? "Oh, you work at Gimbels. I work only three blocks away. We should get together for lunch sometime." As soon as she agrees, be sure to set a firm date. Just because the lunch date is easy come doesn't mean it should be easy go.

If both you and your date can arrange to get more than an hour off from work, a lot of options suddenly become available. You can take in a museum, play Frisbee in the park, go roller-skating, see a movie, take a horse-and-buggy ride . . . the list goes on and on. And because it's a more unusual situation for the typical working woman to find herself in than the conventional dinner date, whatever you end up doing together will seem more spontaneous. You may even find that some of the barriers that existed on a previous evening date don't emerge during this casual, faster-paced experience.

One great variation on the lunch date is the picnic. If you're not the kind of guy who likes to make sandwiches the night before, it's no problem picking up the essentials at a nearby food store or deli on your way to meet your date. Wine, bread, fruit, and cheese make the perfect outdoor fare. Dining together outside is relaxing and romantic, especially in contrast with the stuffy office setting in which most women work.

When you start to think more frequently of lunch as a dating possibility, you'll find yourself with a lot more opportunities for one-on-one interactions with women. It's beneficial to break out of the mode of conceiving of all your dates as Friday or Saturday night affairs anyway, and lunch will provide you with five more golden opportunities a week.

On top of this, you'll find yourself asking out women you would never have thought to ask before. After all, lunch is a lot less of a commitment for you, too. You might not be all that attracted to Myrna, the secretary down the hall, but you might think, *What the hell. I'll give her a thrill and buy her lunch.* It will almost certainly beat the usual sandwich and coffee with the boys. And who knows? Myrna might just turn out to be a lot more interesting and attractive over a chef's salad in a quiet restaurant than she is over her typewriter in the office. Whatever the case, it will be good practice for other dates you go on.

If for reasons of schedule difference a woman can't join you for lunch, make it for a cup of coffee and a snack, or a beer after work. This preserves the essential advantage of the lunch date—its informal spirit.

13

How to Handle a Beautiful Woman

So you want a beautiful woman, huh, one of those slender-waisted, high-breasted ones whose legs look like they come up to just beneath her soft, round bust? One of the ones with long blond hair the color of spun gold; with skin that's smooth and lightly bronzed from the sun; with large, limpid blue eyes; and with pink, plump lips that seem to be inviting you to get lost between them for a lifetime.

Well, terrific then! That's half the battle right there—*admitting* to yourself that you *want* a beautiful woman. A lot of guys feel so totally overwhelmed at the prospect of ever attracting a gorgeous girl that they bullshit themselves with a whole series of excuses—beautiful girls are dumb, frigid, stuck up, only interested in money, have nothing to talk about, are lousy in bed.

All of the above may be true—many beautiful women are limited. Pursued by guys from the time they put on their first training bra, more than a few beautiful women have

never been called upon to develop their other talents—
their warmth, their wit, their sexuality. All they've had to do
is sit back and watch the guys line up for a chance to buy
them a drink.

Just because a great many beautiful women seem passive
and aloof, however, won't stop you from wanting them.
Your attraction is instinctive, genetic. You can't help yourself. God or Darwin or Nature or Whoever gave beautiful
women deliciously curved hips, luscious breasts, and
yummy flat bellies to ensure that men would want to mount
them and make babies, thus preserving the future of the
species. That's why the competition for pretty girls is so
intense. And competition is why a lot of guys give up ahead
of time—they just don't have the stomach, will, or energy to
go after what they really want.

Don't you be one of them.

I'm not saying that a pretty girl is as easy to win as a less
attractive one. But I will tell you this: It takes a lot *less*
energy and guts and drive than you think to capture the
love of a beautiful woman, particularly if you know how to
go about it (which we're going to get to in just another
sentence or two).

Ultimately, of course, you may decide that a woman's
looks are vastly less important than you thought. But at
least if you've had a beautiful woman or two, your opinion
will be based on experience and not just sour grapes.

COUNT YOURSELF IN. The very first thing you have to do to
get a beautiful woman is to get in the game. As with poker,
you can't win the pot unless you're actually sitting down
and playing.

Now I know a lot of you guys may be thinking, *But I don't
really feel like I belong in the game. I'm not good-looking, tall, rich,
funny, or charismatic enough.*

So what? Do it anyway. Make a leap of faith, if only for
me. I'm telling you that you have just as good a chance of

winning a great-looking girl as the next guy, even if *you* don't think you do. So for now, just go along. After all, what do you have to lose?

Okay, then, what exactly do I mean by counting yourself in? Simply this: If you're at a party and there's a breathtakingly lovely creature standing at the punch bowl, stroll over and introduce yourself. Same thing at work. If a terrific-looking brunette has just started work at your office or factory, don't wait around for six months so that all the guys who you think are cooler or handsomer make their moves. Bring the new girl a cup of coffee and introduce yourself, ask her to have lunch, go jogging after work. You needn't propose something heavy and intense, just something that's light and friendly. Even if she declines, you'll have made a statement to the girl, your friends, your co-workers, and, most important, *yourself: You think you're worthy of a good-looking woman.*

Going after what you want, what others want, makes a strong impression on people. It tells them you're a contender, a force to be reckoned with, not just another weakling who's going to stand aside and let others grab all the plums.

Believe me, the mere act of talking to a few beautiful women will have you thinking about yourself in a different light. Suddenly you'll discover that you're not invisible to them, that you're not a nonentity.

I'm not claiming that they'll instantly begin falling all over you (although this has happened to more than a few of my students). I will maintain, however, that the simple process of making contact with pretty girls, no matter on how light and casual a basis, will make having a hot and heavy affair with one seem as if it is now a possibility, not some insanely distant fantasy.

TELL HER SHE'S BRIGHT. Men are always telling pretty girls how pretty they are. And why not? The words come welling up into your mouth as naturally as a belch. *"What pretty lips you have!" "What soft-looking skin!" "Such blue eyes!" "Such lovely hair!"* Sometimes looks are all you can focus on when talking to a good-looking woman.

And let me assure you that there is absolutely nothing to be lost, and perhaps a great deal to be gained, by showering a pretty girl with compliments about her beauty. Despite what some people have written, it is almost impossible to bore a woman with compliments about her looks, no matter how frequently she has heard them. But why not add to your repertoire of positive comments by telling a good-looking woman that she's clever, full of good ideas, witty, brilliant, etc.? These compliments are of a kind that she's not likely to have heard often or possibly at all. But imagine how ego-boosting she will find it to be told how smart she seems, how insightful she is. If there is one area of their development that attractive women are sensitive about, it is their intellect. They are all too familiar with the concept of the dumb blonde, the overdeveloped but undereducated show girl.

Picture how unique and refreshing you will appear then by telling a pretty girl she's bright. I guarantee you, you will make her feel terrific. And when you make someone feel terrific, it's a good bet she'll seek out more of your company. After all, she's thinking maybe you'll make her feel terrific again.

By the way, I discovered this concept of telling pretty women that they're smart shortly after I got out of college. A buddy and I had approached two girls at a bar, one very good-looking, one just kind of average. Since my pal was much taller, somewhat handsomer, and a lot braver than myself, I was sure he was going to wind up with the pretty one. (That's how it usually worked with us.) But that night it was different. The better-looking one gravitated toward me. Several weeks later (we'd begun dating hot and heavy), I asked her why she was drawn to me instead of my more glamorous friend. (This is a dumb question, mind you, and not recommended under any circumstances—it's too much of an admission you don't think you deserve her attention.)

"It was something you said," she replied.

"Something I *said?*" I had no idea what she was talking about.

"Uh-huh. You asked me what I was majoring in; and when I told you math, you said, 'Wow! You must be very bright.' I liked that. Guys are always telling me what great tits I have, but you were the first one to tell me I was smart."

There you have it, right from the horse's mouth. Tell a pretty girl she's bright. Chances are you'll be the first guy to have done so, and chances are she'll like you for it.

ENERGIZE HER. One of the biggest mistakes men make in wooing a pretty woman is to assume that the only way to make an impression on her is to take her out to a big fancy dinner. I guess they figure that everyone else who takes her out must be doing the same thing and that not to spend a fortune on her would be the end of the relationship.

Let me let you in on a little secret. One of the most self-destructive things you can do in pursuing a pretty girl is to think that all you have to do is sit back and take her out to a sumptuous dinner and expensive shows. That's what all your competitors are doing. You'll remind her of everyone else.

No, to take a beautiful woman out on a date that she'll remember over and over, it has to be something that will *energize* her. Consider this: Most beautiful women are rather on the passive side. Everything has come easily to them, been brought to them. They've never felt the need to develop hobbies, fight for friends, reach deep inside to discover hidden talents. Consequently they're often bored. They need a man to fire them up, not set another scene in which all they have to do is sit back and be entertained.

So do it, man. Energize her. Take her roller-skating,

jogging, swimming. Or try horseback riding, a rock concert, white-water rafting, racquetball, hiking, mountain climbing. The point is to aim for something different, active, memorable, participatory—not just an event that's expensive and glamorous but basically passive. A woman who is used to sitting back and being entertained will feel a sense of mastery if you show her how to climb a mountain or skate backward. Her self-esteem, not necessarily any less fragile than that of someone who is not so attractive, will rise. And she will attribute this good feeling, if only subconsciously, to you.

So remember, take a beautiful woman on a date that will fill her with wonder and pride, not soufflés and truffles. She'll like you and, perhaps, eventually love you for it.

GIVE HER SPACE. Okay, I'm going to assume that you've tried some of what I suggested—counted yourself in the running for a pretty woman, told her she was bright, and took her on a date that energized her. And because of all this she's shown some signs of real interest in you. When you called to ask if she wanted to go horseback riding again, she said, "I'd love to!" Or when you stopped by at her desk to see if she needed a ride to the company softball game, she responded, "Terrific. I thought you'd never ask."

Wonderful. But my advice now is not to go all to pieces. Just because a pretty girl has reacted positively to your advances does not necessarily mean that she has fallen desperately in love with you and that you can now drop all restraint on trying to control your attraction to her.

I say this because I understand how strong the temptation may be to fall all over her. Many men, wisely, play it a bit on the cool side in the initial stages of pursuing a particularly attractive woman. They don't want to appear like a love-sick puppy, a stage-door johnny, a helplessly smitten loser. But then as soon as they get the slightest bit of encouragement, they're all over the girl. It is as if they are no longer able to stand the strain—for lo these many weeks or months they have shown sphinxlike patience in waiting for a sign, a nod, a smile. Now that they have it, they misinterpret it. *She loves me! We're an item! We might as well be engaged!*

Nonsense. Remember, this is a beautiful woman we're talking about. Everytime she steps onto an elevator, walks down a supermarket aisle, or sits down at a luncheonette counter, guys will be eyeing her, smiling at her, and hitting up on her. And don't think she's not aware of it. This is a woman with options. She warmed up to you yesterday. Terrific. Now don't spoil it by calling her morning, noon, and night, pleading to be with her.

Keep your own options open. See other women, as many and as often as you can. Your beautiful new girlfriend will sense your outside interests and be curious. Wait five or seven or a dozen days before you call her again. Yes, you like her and are glad she seems to like you back. But that doesn't mean you're going to drop the entire ninety-eight percent of the rest of your life in order to devote full time to her.

Remember, the most critical element in winning a beautiful woman is being unique. Let the other guys throw themselves at her feet. It's true you're attracted to her. But it's not like you've been waiting for her for your whole life. You've got other interests as well.

Can *you* meet, date, and love a beautiful woman? I'm absolutely sure of it. You just have to count yourself in and follow the above techniques. It may take a little time, practice, and guts. But I'll bet before long you'll be squiring around the woman of your dreams.

14

Great Dates
That Keep a Woman
Coming Back for More

I'm going to presume that your perseverance with a hard-to-get woman has paid off. Your occasional lunch dates have nurtured her feelings for you to the point where she's now willing to see you at night.

Now the problem is, what the hell are you going to do with her? Because let's face it, how you take a woman out for your first big evening together often defines the entire future of your relationship with her. Take her for a slice of pizza, and unless she's helplessly attracted to you she may think to herself, *Hmm, this guy has about as much élan as a wastebasket.* On the other hand, take her to the best restaurant in town for dinner and a good bottle of wine, and she may decide you're a real romantic prospect.

I can hear your outraged reaction already. "Take her to the best restaurant in town? Why should I waste my hard-earned money on some dame I hardly know? And besides, my friend Iggy, he never buys a woman nothing and he's up to his neck in girls."

Listen, we all have a friend Iggy, and—for some reason I'll never understand—the worse he treats women, the more they seem attracted to him. All I know is, I'm no Iggy. And you're probably not, either. Only about one man in twenty is. And if you're not born an Iggy, it's unlikely that you can learn how to become one. So give up on any notion of trying to make it big with women by being a bastard. For one thing, it's probably not as much fun as it looks. For another, I bet you'll find that taking women out on dates that are classy, different, exotic, and memorable will lead to a love life that is every bit as busy as Iggy's, if not more so.

I interviewed a couple of dozen of hip, pretty, articulate women to find out the best dates they ever went on. I culled out the dates that seemed as if they'd be the most effective and then tossed in a few favorites of my own. True, some of them are extravagant and may run you a few bucks. But you've got a lot more disposable income at this stage in your life than some poor bastard who's bogged down with a wife and a couple of kids. So spend it while you can. My grandpa Sig always said, "Some men live within their means; others decide how they want to live, then go out and earn enough money to live that way."

Dinner in a Distant City

On weekends, round-trip plane fare for two between New York and Washington, D.C., is $116. Between Los Angeles and San Francisco, the fare for you and a date will run you a mere $220. And between Madison, Wisconsin, and Chicago it's $272. Granted, none of the above fares is chicken feed. But think how easy it is these days to blow a hundred dollars on a pair of shoes you didn't need, a doo-dad for your car, a couple of wasted nights in a singles bar.

Also, think how impressed your new lady friend will be when you head your car out to the municipal airport.

"Where are we going?" she'll want to know.

"Oh, no place special," you'll reply nonchalantly. "A little seafood restaurant in New Orleans. They've got the greatest stone crabs in the world there, much better than any you can get here in Houston."

Whether this is true or not is a moot point. How many other guys have ever had the originality to fly her four hundred miles and back just for dinner? It's a date she'll remember for a lifetime and be able to brag to her girlfriends and parents about. And the more she talks about it, the bigger and bolder a hero you'll become.

"He flew you to Houston just for dinner!?" her friends'll squeal. "He sounds terrific."

"He is!" she'll reply.

And if the tab for such an evening still has you concerned, console yourself with this. If the restaurant you eat at in a distant city isn't all that grand, no matter. The trip is the important thing. Perhaps if you'd stayed local you would have felt obligated to dine at a more luxurious, expensive eatery. Naturally, the savings won't be enough to offset the cost of the flight, but it can certainly help a bit. And believe me, the extra dollars will be more than worth it in the impression you'll make.

A Japanese Meal in a Private Room

If you decide to dine locally instead of jet out of town, I would strongly recommend a romantic Japanese meal. Japanese restaurants are proliferating across the country, and with good reason. The food is reasonably priced, low in calories and fat content, and often superb.

In many of the Japanese restaurants in my section of the country, New York, there are private rooms in the back in which regular customers dine shoeless while sitting on pillows on the floor. It is often difficult to get one of these rooms if you walk straight in off the street, but I'm sure if you call a couple of days ahead of time you can reserve a private room for just you and your date.

I think you'll love the intimacy and coziness of dining Japanese style. There is something about eating with your shoes off on pillows on the floor that automatically brings you closer to your date. And of course this is heightened by the two of you being alone in a quaint, bamboo-curtained room. Make sure you order lots of hot sake and cold beer to loosen her inhibitions as well as your own. You will find your waitress quiet and discreet, which, given the intimacy of the setting, may be terribly important.

Wine Tasting

Most everyone has seen an announcement for a wine tasting in a liquor store or restaurant. But how many of us have ever been to one?

I attended my first several years ago, and it was wonderful. The crowd was small and well dressed. There was a pleasant hushed friendliness to the conversation. Even though most in attendance hadn't known each other previously, they seemed immediately comfortable and interested in one another's company. Perhaps it was a shared love of wine that drew us all closer together.

I found the proceedings truly revelatory, and the constant sipping of fine wines a treat. And of course it wasn't long before all the guests had a nice little buzz on.

Imagine how impressed and entertained a date of yours would be if you brought her to an affair like this rather than an ordinary movie or disco. The mere act of having *thought* of a wine tasting marks you as a classy, cultivated guy. And the reality of the experience—the elegant, carpeted room; the refined, accomplished crowd; the delicious, relaxing wines—will put you over the top. Simply stop off at a liquor store on your way back to her place and pick up a bottle, or a couple for that matter, of the wine she and you liked best.

Another nice feature of wine tastings, by the way, is that they rarely cost more than ten to fifteen dollars per person and almost always have excellent cheeses and crackers as appetizers.

Work Out Together

If you like racquetball, squash, pumping iron, stretching, swimming, or exercising in any other fashion suitable to the new kind of indoor health clubs popping up all over the place these days, you might invite a woman to work out with you.

The tennis and racquet and fitness clubs I've been to lately are downright spiffy and usually equipped with everything from trampolines to whirlpools. A friend tells me that she recently was invited out on a first date to play squash. Afterward she and her man sat in the sauna together. When they'd worked up a good sweat, he asked her if she wanted to cool off in the pool.

"But I don't have a bathing suit," she replied.

"So I'll buy you one," he said. And he did, springing for a serviceable twenty-five-dollar tank suit.

My friend said her date's generosity was the perfect topper to an already terrific evening. The squash was exhilarating—much better than sitting around over a gooey, calorie-packed meal in a smoke-filled restaurant. The sauna was cozy and sexy. And the pool was bracing and refreshing. After a light salad and a bottle of wine, they went back to her place and had a workout of a far different kind.

You might find your date is similarly exhilarated by a coed visit to a health club, what with all the healthy, scantily clad bodies about.

How do you find out if she's into sports? When you call for a date, just ask. "Do you play tennis? Squash? Work out on the universal machine?" If she says yes, then simply search out a modern-looking fitness club and tell the manager you want to stop by for a trial visit. Then proceed as described above. If she isn't a fitness buff, then try the following super date.

Rent a Rolls

Uh oh, you're probably thinking, *here he goes again with one of those wipe-you-out-flat-broke ideas again.*

Not necessarily. I just got off the phone with a local place that leases Rolls-Royces and other exotic cars, and there you can rent a 1950 Silver Wraith for twenty-five dollars an hour. What about taking a woman to the drive-in cinema in one? If you keep the car for three hours, that comes out to seventy-five bucks. The drive-in itself will only be another five to ten. Now I admit, it's not exactly price-competitive with an evening of bowling and beer; but tell me if it won't make a wee bit more of a statement about what kind of guy you are?

Take Her Dancing

There are a multitude of good reasons to ask women out on dancing dates, so don't try to remember them all. Just remember to do it.

First of all, when you ask a woman out on a dancing date you double the likelihood that she'll go out with you, since many women who love to dance won't go out alone for fear of being bombarded by hordes of men. An escort, even one they know only slightly, eliminates this problem for them. Since many men don't think to ask women to go out dancing, your proposal could be a real treat—something long hoped for.

Second, taking a woman out dancing indicates to her that you're somebody a little bit special, not the typical male whose idea of a good time is beer and hot dogs at a ball game. You're someone with grace, culture, and a better understanding of women. And some other important qualities besides.

"Men who like to dance are more sensuous," Jeanne, a sexy New York City actress, told me. "Not only have I found from experience that they're better in bed, they're more fun to go places and do things with in general. They have more zest for life. I always want to know if a man likes to dance before I get involved with him. I think, hey, if I can enjoy dancing with this guy, I can probably enjoy doing other things with him as well."

Dancing dates are especially important in the early stages of a relationship, because they allow a lot of touching to occur. (It's the fastest socially acceptable way to get your hands on a woman.) Or if you're in a relationship that has grown a little stagnant, dancing is a great way to give it a fresh burst of life. Megan, who met her boyfriend Roger at an Ivy League university a few years ago, told me, "Dancing is an aphrodisiac. If we go out dancing together it's just assumed that we're going to make love when we come home."

An Art Gallery Opening

An opening or first night of any kind has an aura of drama about it that can add tremendous sparkle and excitement to all your first dates. How do you get invited to art gallery openings? Just visit an art gallery, or a whole bunch of them, and ask to be put on their mailing lists. I get invited to openings from galleries I haven't been in since 1975.

The nice thing about a gallery opening is the crowd. It usually consists of artists, writers, journalists, bohemian-looking women in exotic, erotic outfits, and jet-setty couples with money. Wine and cheese, sometimes hard liquor, and occasionally champagne are provided free. And of course there is no admission fee either, the hope being that the gallery will make money by selling a couple of paintings.

To have had the cultivation and intelligence and aware-ness to get invited to a gallery opening will say a myriad of good things about you to your date, not the least of which is that you certainly seem to hang out with an interesting crowd. Even if you don't know a soul there, you will find that those in attendance are easy to approach and to talk to. If your date isn't looking, perhaps you can even collect a telephone number or two. Arty women are often striking and adventurous.

By the way, if your date remarks upon a photograph or painting that is exceedingly reasonable, say around twenty dollars, you may want to buy it for her. It's a grand gesture, and the gift is one she will remember you by for a lifetime. For even if she winds up living with or marrying someone else, she will always have this memento *you* bought her hanging on the wall of her home, perhaps even her bed-room. Art is something people just don't throw out.

Bring Her a Present

Again I'm recommending you spend money. But again I do it because it makes sense. Although this is supposedly the age of women's liberation, dutch treating, and women opening doors and lighting cigarettes for themselves, the truth is *most* women still prefer to be treated gallantly, to be taken care of.

In the research I did while putting together *How to Pick Up Women*, dozens of women told me nothing puts them off more than a man who glances over nervously at every click of the cab meter, suspiciously eyes the higher-priced items on the menu, or clears his throat with displeasure when his date orders a Chivas Regal on the rocks. These same women also claim that nothing is more relaxing or makes them feel more taken care of than when they are in the company of a man who seems able and willing to pay for whatever costs pop up while he and his date are out together.

The point of this is not that you should write a blank check to hand to every woman you date and say, "Spend, go ahead, whatever you want." That's not my point at all. What I am trying to impress upon you is that a woman will view your generosity as a sign of love, of caring, of giving— not as a sign of weakness or foolishness, not as a tip-off that you are someone to be taken advantage of. Nor will she assume that your generosity is endless or bottomless, a perpetual state that will exist for every moment the two of you are together. She will see it more as a sign of courtship, a gesture that you want very badly to get to know her, to have her like you.

Most women are fully aware that men go out of their way at the beginning of a relationship in order to capture a woman's attention and affection. Women do the same. There is a realization that the rich life cannot last forever. That's okay. The very fact that a man extended himself in the first place is often more than enough to attract a woman and make her interested. Because it shows *you* are interested.

Witness the following case. A woman friend who is now happily married described her very first date with a struggling student. When he arrived at her apartment door, he had a tiny gift-wrapped box in his hand. "This is for you," he said.

"For me? But why? You hardly know me."

"Because I was very excited about seeing you," he replied. "I just felt like it."

Inside the little box was a pair of inexpensive but pretty Indian earrings. My friend reports that the gift made her feel so *liked* and *wanted* that she almost started crying.

"Men don't realize how tough it is to be a woman living alone in a big city," she says. "There was always so much for me to be suspicious of, so many people trying to take advantage of me. When somebody does something genuinely nice and loving for you, it makes you like them back tremendously." Apparently so. She wound up marrying the man who gave her the earrings.

Can you do the same? Of course you can. Next time you arrive to pick up your date, see how delighted she is because you've brought her a book you enjoyed, some flowers, a box of candy, even a card you thought was funny or clever. Or better yet, if the two of you happen to be window-shopping, take her inside and buy her a belt, a hat, a scarf, or even a scandalous pair of panties. I suspect that at a later time in the evening, or a date or two hence, she'll be more than happy to model them for you.

Brunch

If you live in a city, even a small one, you've probably noticed that many nice pubs have Sunday morning breakfasts. These are often the best buy in town. Fresh orange juice, Bloody Marys, pancakes, sausages, omelets, eggs Benedict—you name it, they've got it, and often at a ridiculously low price. So here's an idea. If you've just met a woman that you want to ask out, why not make it for Sunday breakfast? She'll be impressed. First, because it's a little unusual. Second, because it says you're not desperate. You didn't ask her out for the big one, Saturday night. And third, it indicates you're willing to take your time with her. After all, you don't usually hit up on a girl to come home to bed with you in the middle of the day.

Many women these days tell me they are sick and tired of guys trying to hustle them into the sack only hours after first meeting. They say if they do give in, they do it only to hold on to the man, never because they look forward to the instant sex. I suspect a lot of men are similarly motivated. They push for quick sex only to chalk up a new conquest, not because they really enjoy the sex.

So why not be different? Different to a woman often means *special*. And special men are the kind women fall in love with.

Is there a nice restaurant, hotel, or pub near you that serves a lush, generous Sunday brunch? Hell, man, take advantage of it. You ought to have a different brunch part-ner at least several times a month. I think you'll find these midmorning meals are a wonderfully relaxed, casual, hip, and modern way in which to get to know someone slowly but surely, which is often the best way of all. Then when the two of you do get into bed, you can really have a super time together.

The Great Outdoors

Ask a woman what places she considers sexy or romantic and few will tell you "a nice bedroom" or "Plato's Retreat." No, the answers you'll hear (and I know, because I've heard them) are "a deserted beach," "a sunny meadow," or even "the top of a mountain." By and large it's the outdoors that most women associate with *l'esprit d'amour*.

So why not make your next date with a woman a picnic in the park, a stroll along the river, a visit to a scenic flower garden, or a horseback ride through backwoods trails (as-suming you can ride, of course)?

Any of these will mark you as a man who is unique and adventurous, for they will set you apart from the droves of men who can never think of any place to take a woman but to dinner or the flicks.

You've probably observed that most, if not all, of the ten dates described above are different and unique. There's a reason for that. Women like men who are special. They remember them better and have vastly more romantic daydreams and fantasies about them. To take a woman out on a magical, memorable date is a way for a man who isn't all that good-looking or successful to win out over a man who is. It's also a way to turn on and intrigue a woman who accepted a date with you more because she didn't have anything to do that weekend than because she found you maddeningly attractive. In short, to take a woman out on a spectacular date is a way to keep her coming back for more dates. So my hope is that you're not just going to get excited over the ideas in this book, but that you're actually going to go out and try some of them. Because believe me, they work. And not only are they enthralling to the women you're with, but *you'll* have a good time as well. Which is kind of what good dating is all about—the *both* of you having fun.

15

How to Talk to Women

The strong, silent type may look good on the silver screen, but in real life it's usually the guy with the gift of gab who gets the girl.

Let me take you back a few years. When I was with a girl during my high school years, I always tried very hard not to speak to her unless she spoke to me first. "Shebakian" was okay in answer to the question "Who do you have for American history?" But "What a lovely day!" volunteered totally on my own was verboten; it was a sign, in my eyes anyway, of weakness and gabbiness. After all, talking was feminine in those days, something girls did with each other *ad nauseam* over the phone.

Real men, on the other hand, used words only when they had to. If a fellow had any doubts, all he had to do was go out to the flicks and watch the likes of Eastwood, Bronson, and McQueen—men of few words, all of them—silently smash a few bad guys into submission. And when they were

done, they got the girl, of course—not by wooing or courting or dressing up or putting on deodorant or doing any of
those other things men do to please women, but simply by
standing around looking macho and sullen. They got girls
in real life as well—you could see pictures of them festoon-
ing the pages of the *National Enquirer* while squiring beauties like Jill Ireland, Ali MacGraw, supermodel Barbara
Minty, and so on. The message Hollywood was sending
out, and in many ways is *still* sending out, is that *women like
men who don't say much.*

You know what my reaction is to that? Bullshit!

If there's one half of the human race that is particularly
susceptible to the magic of language, it's women. Say the
right words to them, and I swear to you that you can get
them to do just about anything you want. The following
stories, all true, illustrate my point.

Item 1: A man got into bed with the girl who lived with
him. She was furious. They had just returned home from a
party where he had been flirting with another girl so outra-
geously that his own girlfriend was making not-so-veiled
threats about moving out. Naturally, as he pulled the covers
over them, our hero could sense that his lady was hardly in
the mood to make love. He did not let this get in his way.

"You looked great tonight," he said. "Very sexy."

"Yeah, well if I looked so damn sexy how come you were
paying so much attention to that Anita slut?"

"I wasn't the only one who thought you looked hot. Jim
Tuttle told me he thinks you have a terrific ass." (Notice
how he totally sidestepped her question.)

"He did not."

"I swear it. And I saw Harry and Ralph trying to look up
your legs when you were sitting on the couch. Guys always
get turned on when you wear that purple dress."

"Are you just saying that?"

"What would I make something like that up for? It makes

me jealous knowing that half the guys there tonight wanted to get into your pants."

"Oh, come on."

"I'm serious, for Christ's sake. I could see guys eyeing you all night long." Here he reached over and put his hand on her belly. She let him. "I guess it's something you just can't hide. Men must sense how incredibly sexy and juicy you are." At this point our hero discovered his girlfriend wasn't angry anymore.

Item 2: A woman was having dinner out with a man to whom she was not in the least bit attracted. She had accepted a date with him only because she had nothing else to do that night, he had asked her out three times in a row without her saying yes, and he had promised to take her to a particularly nice restaurant. During the course of the meal the man kept on staring at her in wonder, as if smitten beyond embarrassment, beyond his control.

Finally, he spoke—shyly at first, then with more and more passion. "I'm sorry I keep staring at you like this, but I can't help myself. Your skin is so perfect, so smooth. I keep on thinking how incredible it must be to wake up next to someone like you, to be close to you. It makes me almost dizzy to imagine what it would be like to make love to you, how incredibly excited I would feel knowing that for once in my life I was going to touch someone who was so phenomenally beautiful. I mean, I wouldn't even have to do it again . . . it would be like having the fantasy of a lifetime come true."

At first the woman was only mildly amused. As he went on, though, she actually felt herself becoming aroused by the image he was creating for her, the sight of her own soft curves beneath the sheets, her hair spread out on her pillow. And to think how appreciative he was of her beauty, her femininity. How in awe he was of her! Could she let the poor fellow down? Absolutely not! She took him home and let him make love to her, endulging him, for this one evening anyway, by making his fantasy come true. What a sense of power it gave her!

Item 3: A man was sitting in a pub with an extremely attractive woman with long blond hair and large soft lips. This was their tenth date in six months, and it was turning out exactly like the nine before it—lots of polite formal chatter about politics, books, and the movie they had just seen. The man was hoping it would not end as the previous nine had, with nothing more than a platonic good-night kiss. Yet he could not think of a way to break the pattern, to get the conversation onto a livelier, more personal level. *What the hell's the matter with me?* he thought. *With my friends I'm funny and sarcastic and entertaining, a terrific storyteller, full of clever one-liners. With this woman I'm a dud, dull and pompous. How come I can't be more interesting?*

Meanwhile, the woman was telling him about an uncle of hers who was principal of a local high school. His name rang a bell. "You mean old White Shoulders Peterson," blurted out the man.

The woman looked shocked. "White Shoulders?"

"Well, yeah," explained her date, "on account of he always wore these blue shirts and had so much dandruff. Gee, I'm sorry," he apologized. "I didn't know he was your uncle."

But the woman was laughing her head off. "Boy, if Uncle Ted knew that was his nickname, he would have died."

"Hell, that's nothing. You should have seen my imitation of him."

"Go ahead."

"Nah, you wouldn't like it."

"Are you kidding? Even my cousins make fun of Uncle Ted."

The man let himself be coaxed into his impression, pressing his jaw against his chest to give the appearance of several extra chins and spitting as he spoke. His date nearly collapsed on the table. "God, you've got him down perfect," she howled.

And that was all it took. From then on the couple began recalling dozens of stories from high school—the food fight at the sports banquet, the planned coughing during assemblies, and countless other incidents. When our hero kissed the girl good night, this after each of them had knocked down half a dozen beers, it was an entirely different story from the old peck on the side of the face. In fact the kiss didn't end really until the next morning when she got up and made him breakfast. And all because he made fun of her uncle.

Well, now, what conclusions can we draw from the above? The most obvious is that many women like to be told that they are beautiful and sexy. It's fine to come right out with it—"You're beautiful and sexy"—but even better if you can do it with a little artistry, a little inventiveness.

In *Item 1,* the man quoted *other* men to add a touch of originality to his compliment. This is often particularly effective because many, and perhaps most, women fantasize being attractive not to one but to entire legions of men. In Nancy Friday's wonderful book on women's fantasies, *My Secret Garden,* there must be several dozen in which women describe themselves being ogled by groups of men at parties, parades, football stadiums, etc.

The reason I feel it's so important to stress this aspect of a woman's fantasy life is that it seems to be different from that of most men's. If a woman told you her three roommates all thought you were good-looking, you'd most certainly be flattered. But would it actually arouse you? And would you have chosen it as a fantasy? Probably not. Yet if you were to tell your date that all of the guys down at the shop where you work as a car mechanic were sitting around the other day and decided that she had the best ass of all the women residing in the middle-Atlantic states, that very comment might very well make her feel sexy and inclined to be touched and stroked. The image of half a dozen men discussing her wonderful derriere would be enough to get her glands going. So don't just chuckle to yourself and then neglect to file this information away where you can call upon it at will. It can come in handy.

In *Item 2*, the man under discussion gave poetic voice to some strong feelings that were welling up inside him. And he was right on the mark, for two reasons. One is that he made the woman feel incredibly special. He didn't just have a crush on her; he *worshiped* her. Second, he was lyrical rather than crude in his description of her body.

As frequently as you may read in sleazy novels and in letters to sexology magazines about women who thrill to being bombarded with a tirade of expletives while they are being made love to, the truth is most women really prefer gentler, more elegant language. Yes, a woman enjoys being informed she has great tits. But she'd much rather have you put it like this: "Your breasts are so soft and gentle-looking, so beautifully shaped, they look like they were created by some fabulous sculptor, someone who was putting together the perfect woman." And though it helps if you *really* feel this way, you can also succeed even at those times when you aren't quite as moved as you sound.

What women like is to be adored, and often the very *act* of adoring them is enough to carry the day. As many women have told me, "It's okay if a guy is bullshitting. At least he's taken the trouble to do that. Like when you're in Rome, and all those Italian guys come up to you and give you the you-are-so-beautiful line. *'Bella, bella, cara mia.'* You know they're slinging it, but you don't care. Most American guys just stand there trying to look tough."

On the other hand, if you really do feel it, let the words at the tip of your tongue take flight. So many men suppress their poetic impulses because they fear they'll sound weak or feminine. They feel that Bronson or Eastwood wouldn't be caught dead uttering such gushy sweet nothings. Well, I'm not sure about Charles or Clint, but I can give you some inside dope on the Duke. Back in 1977 and 1978, we spent quite a bit of time together writing and shooting commercials and playing chess during breaks. And John Wayne, the Quiet Man—literally—of Film, was a prodigious talker in the flesh. He loved women and words and Shakespeare and cut flowers and good books and was as eloquent and chatty around the girls as any guy I know. And hell, if he didn't feel embarrassed about speaking from the heart, then why should you?

One final point. In *Item 3,* our hero first broke the ice with his date when he stopped being so damn polite. Falling into the role of goody-goody when with a woman is something that afflicts millions of otherwise funny, irreverent men, and I'm not really sure why. But I do know how to fight it. Tell her a joke. Or tell her she's special or sexy or pretty. Pretend for a minute that she's your best buddy, or your sister, someone you feel really comfortable with, and then tell her something you'd tell them.

And if all else fails, discuss your problem with her. Say, "Carol, I don't know why this happens, but whenever we're together I get very serious and formal around you. I start talking about things like El Salvador and the prime rate, which is okay, but I'd really much rather talk about how we feel about each other." I think you'll find that most women will take you up on this in an instant.

Do you get tongue-tied around women because you're afraid it's weak to talk too much? Do you muzzle yourself when you feel an urge to tell a girl you think she's pretty or you like being with her? Are you afraid you'll sound corny or manipulative by telling a woman she's a great beauty, a work of art?

Don't. Take it from me, the guys who do best with

women talk to them—plenty—in the most personal, intimate way. If you can do that, looks and money couldn't be less important. Why, even a fellow with a schnozz like Cyrano de Bergerac can find romance.

16

How to Keep a Date from Ending

It's eleven o'clock on a Friday night, and what should be a dream come true is rapidly turning into the biggest letdown of your life. The date you've dreamed about for months is going to fizzle out before midnight.

First, it took you almost two months just to work up the courage to ask Suzanne out. After all, you had never gone out before with a girl even nearly as good-looking as she is. And the competition for her at the office was intense ever since the day she arrived. Your timing had to be just right, you told yourself.

Then, when much to your surprise she accepted your invitation, she got sick a few days later. Your date had to be postponed for a week. You thought perhaps that was a ploy, Suzanne's cryptic attempt to weasel out of going out with you. But no, the extra week passed, and lo and behold Suzanne even came up to you to ask if the date was still on.

Now here you are, having had dinner and seen a film, and

the digits on your watch read only 11:17. As you walk toward your car, you're not even holding hands, and there's a strange blankness in the air. What's going to happen now? You're not simply going to drive her home, shake her hand, and say, "See you at work on Monday"? Surely the evening won't come to that uninspired a finale!

No, life could not be that cruel—unless you wanted it to be. You owe it to yourself, and to Suzanne, to make the night into something more, to bring adventure, daring, and romance into it. And there's something else you want to accomplish, too. You want you and Suzanne to get to know each other a little bit. That's why you asked her out in the first place.

Dinner and a movie are fine as far as they go, but for a first date you need something more to bring you closer together. What you've done so far can be considered the foreplay of the evening . . . It would be an awful big tease to end right here.

But, Eric, I hear your silent thoughts in the fictional tableau I've created, *Suzanne looks tired. And I'm not even sure she's having a good time. Maybe I should just drive her home.*

Nonsense. Suzanne looks tired because she's just sat for four hours. The night is still young. And besides, the whole point of going out on a weekend is to be able to stay up and go a little bit wild.

Now, about Suzanne's response to the evening so far—it is almost undoubtedly the same as yours. You've been a little bit nervous, and so has she. You enjoyed dinner and the movie, and so did she. Now you're both wondering what's going to happen next. But it's up to you to do something about it.

Why me? you protest. *Doesn't Suzanne have a say?* Of course she does. But you're the one who proposed the date, you're the one who engineered and financed it, and now you must be the one to keep it going. Like it or not, you are in a leadership position. Accept this fact, and you've got the key to making your dates successful.

Particularly in the early stages of a relationship, women do not want to be asked what kind of a date they'd like to go on, how long it should last, and questions of that nature. They want the evening *orchestrated* for them.

So, maestro, here's what you do. Take Suzanne by her pretty hand and, depending on where you are, what you know about Suzanne's personality, and your own interests, propose one of the following:

• Going to a disco, country music bar, or some other place to dance. This is especially revitalizing.

• Getting some form of exercise. In the summer many tennis courts are lit late into the night, or there may be an outdoor pool or lake to swim in. In the winter you might find that some health clubs (especially in the larger cities) stay open late on certain nights with swimming pools, saunas, and other facilities available. Research this in advance.

• Stopping in on a party that a friend of yours is throwing. Your date will appreciate being introduced to a new crowd of people.

• Checking out a late-night comedy routine. Don't forget, laughter is about the best relaxer.

• Taking a walk. You can do this in either the city or the country. There's nothing like a good stretch of the legs, and as you're walking around you'll probably get ideas for other things to do.

• Going to a coffee shop to get tea or coffee and dessert. You may find a place where a guitar being gently strummed provides the background music. This scores extra points for romance.

• Taking a drive to "Lookout Point," a romantic spot with a great view. I even know of one fellow who keeps a telescope in his back seat to make the suggestion of star watching more plausible. He also keeps a bottle of wine in his front seat, however, to pass the time if the night is too cloudy to pretend to see constellations.

• Going to the top of the tallest building in town, such as the World Trade Center, in New York, for a cocktail. This is the city equivalent of "Lookout Point." The dramatic view is well worth the extra buck or so you may pay for a drink. This is especially effective if the woman has never been to the place before.

• Going back to your place for dessert, a game of chess, a joint, music, a look at your art prints, and so on. Always keep a bottle of champagne in your fridge for this eventuality. Nothing can give an evening that extra touch of class better than for you to casually pull a bottle of bubbly out and toast the evening.

Now keep in mind that these activities are not mutually exclusive. As a matter of fact, they complement one another. For instance, going back to your place to give her a massage will seem a lot more natural proposition if you've just discoed for two hours. A rule of thumb is that it's good to get some kind of physical release in, such as by dancing, walking, or swimming, before you settle down for a long period of sitting around, talking, or otherwise being intimate.

The best dates aren't always the longest ones, but intimacy usually does increase as an evening progresses. Only if your date specifically requests to get home should you feel compelled to terminate an evening together . . . and even then you can try to extend it with some out-of-the-blue, last-minute proposal. Keep in mind that the same woman who makes you stutter at nine o'clock may make you feel like the biggest stud on Earth three hours later. It's worth giving your evening that much of a chance to progress.

So remember, if you don't want a date to end, don't let it

end. Keeping things moving is the simple trick that allows you to do this.

Taking Your Time

Before we get into the nitty-gritty of how to take a woman to bed, I want to make one point absolutely clear: Success with women is not getting as many into bed as soon as possible.

We live in a very achievement-oriented society. Even as children we are instructed to get the best grades, make the most friends, be the best athlete. Directly or indirectly, we are continually asked to prove ourselves. Unfortunately, this carries over into our relationships with women.

If you're like most guys, you probably saw a lot of spy and secret-agent movies growing up. You may still watch them. Even though you know they are just movies, they affect you. You witness an unusually handsome man of superior wit, intelligence, and athletic prowess defeat the Russians or some deadly evil genius for the sake of the free world. And in the process, usually as an essential component of it, take a lot of different women to bed.

This man is heroic to you. You want to be like him.

Unfortunately, you don't live in the make-believe world that the James Bonds and Simon Templars do. Your suit isn't an arsenal in disguise, you don't have a black belt in seven martial arts, and you don't save the world from evil totalitarian schemes on a weekly basis.

Oh, and one more thing. You don't have hundreds of incredibly desirable, exotic women magically falling into your arms. One or two, maybe. But not hundreds.

Still, the heroic impulse dies hard. You may admit to not having the vehicle for being a full-blown hero—no superweapons, spy skills, or secret mission to accomplish—but there is one area in which you'd like to think of yourself as the equal of one of these chaps. As a lover. Because it's their sexual magnetism and savvy that really seem to set them apart, that qualify them as worthy of everything else we give them credit for. Yes, quite clearly the message these movies convey is this: The essence of superiority is sexual superiority. That's why their opponents are so ugly no girl would ever touch them.

But that gives sexual prowess more importance than it really merits. It is not the be-all and end-all of who one is. Sex should not be a way to prove yourself. Ideal sex is a function of fun and love, not competition.

Think of the women! They don't want to be a prop in somebody else's private movie. They don't want to be merely a way for a would-be hero to justify himself. And that's why they won't cooperate when this kind of vibe comes across. They want to be appreciated for who *they* are, to be made to feel special even in the ordinary, mundane world we actually do live in. Which is an assignment you've never seen James Bond have to execute.

I'll let you in on a secret. The way to real success with women is to give up the phony models that Hollywood and Madison Avenue throw at you to emulate. Coolness does not win affection or even admiration. Neither does machismo. Tenderness and sensitivity do.

Another negative force to deal with is peer pressure. A friend tells you—brags really—that not only is his girlfriend great in bed, but she told him that he is, too! There's a conversation in the locker room about how many girls someone screwed over the weekend. The guys at work make a bet who can get to the new receptionist the quickest. All this is fun and has a humorous tone. You want to be able to participate in it, to be one of the gang, a man among men. You want to have your own stories to tell.

There are two important facts to keep in mind with regard to the "locker-room" macho approach to women. The first is that most of the stories you hear are either exaggerated or made up. They usually are told because somebody feels insecure and needs a way to feel big. And the truth of the matter is, you can't screw your way to importance anyway.

The second thing to keep in mind is that not too many real ladies' men spend a lot of time talking about their exploits. One reason is that they don't consider them exploits in the first place. They're not taking advantage of women, they're showing them a good time. And why should they talk about it anyway? They've got all the security and ego gratification they need. When it comes to winning with women, there's a real dichotomy between people who talk and people who do.

The basic message here is that you shouldn't let the media, acquaintances, or even your good friends make you feel unnecessarily pressured to get laid. Racking up the score should never be what motivates you to take a woman to bed. That attitude backfires nine times out of ten. A woman can sense it, feel it in her bones. She wants sex just as much as you do, but she doesn't want to be rushed into it. She wants coming together to be a slow process. And she's right. Sex is better that way.

Now I know that it's not entirely correct to attribute the typical male's overeagerness to get a woman into bed to purely cultural factors. There's one more pressure that I haven't talked about yet—and that's plain, simple horniness. I'm sure you know the feeling. It's the electric shock that races through your body when a woman smiles at you sexily, the rush of blood that occurs when you accidentally touch thighs with a woman, the tightening of your stomach and tingling of your ears that a mere caress can induce when done by the right female. It's the state of more or less constant tension and excitement that almost all males under the age of eighty live in.

Yes, horniness is a fact of life. But that doesn't mean it has to be *the* fact of life. It has to be kept under control.

The irony behind being *obviously* horny is that you rarely

get laid by being that way. The more desperate you seem for sex, the less a woman will want to have it with you. The same principle applies on a purely social level; women do not want to be with men who appear desperate for their company or for their approval. So the message to put across to a woman is "I want you," not "I need you."

There's a logic to this. A woman wants to feel that she's unique, that you're not just interested in her because she's a female of the species. Anyone who seems obsessed with his own desire or need probably can't do her justice, probably can't relax enough to truly take in her finer points. She wants someone who will savor her, moment by moment and kiss by kiss. "After all," as Janet, a New York City fashion model put it, "this is not the hundred-yard dash we're doing."

So show your self-control, and make sure that your girl-friend knows that what she is witnessing is self-control, not disinterest or passivity. This doesn't mean that you shouldn't be direct. It means that you should choose your moment and method of being direct carefully. Build up to it . . . slowly . . . calmly . . . romantically.

For a woman, nothing is more important than having a man take his time. Unfortunately, this is not the usual be-havior she encounters. Most men bombard women with sexual demands, if not by directly asking for sex—which is better—than by acting sullen and withdrawn until they get what they're after.

Most women correctly read this as sexual anxiety and insecurity, not simply lust. It's a real turnoff. Sometimes they'll go ahead and have sex with a guy just to calm him down, to make him feel better about himself. But the sex is not very good, and her having been more or less pressured into it undermines the relationship in other ways.

Think of courtship and seduction as related arts. They bring you forward into intimacy without creating tension. And they share a central dynamic—a slow pace. This is the course that the skilled lover takes. He knows that when he finally does come out with all guns firing he'll have a willing target.

The advantages of taking your time are numerous. It distinguishes you from the herd of men stampeding after sex. It suggests to a woman that you're a skilled lover, whether you are or not. And it allows you to get to know a woman in a relaxed way so that the sex you eventually do have together will be of a much higher quality. In the world of winning with women, it is one of the best techniques there is.

Fellas, in the course of your life you're going to have more carnal capers, more wild and orgiastic experiences than you can even conceive right now. So don't push, push, push. Persistence is important, but so is patience. Let your relationships evolve slowly, let your women feel unpressured to have a good time. Let other guys feel a need to prove themselves. You'll get your share of sex. And then some.

17

From Talking to Touching

But I've been taking my time, a lot of you may be thinking, *which was all very fine when I was getting to know her. But now I'm stuck in a rut. I can't seem to cross the bridge from conversation to consummation.*

This is not an uncommon problem. I suffered from it myself in my late teens and early twenties, and in recent years I have been consulted by literally hundreds of men who feel overly inhibited about first reaching out to touch a woman. Of course just because other men share your problem, doesn't make it any easier to live with. After all, what could be more frustrating than to have blown your Saturday night and half of your paycheck and to have got no more contact out of it than the proverbial handshake? For the eleventh date in a row?

A polite "thank you" or "I had a very nice time" is just not much of a memory to sustain you through a long, lonely night. If you do have to go home alone, you at least want to be able to recall how pleasant it was to have walked through the city hand in hand, with periodic affectionate hugs, her pretty face reaching up to kiss you, and all the other delights of intimacy.

And why shouldn't you? There's a lot of contact to be had in this world, and women are as frustrated not to have it as you are. Nothing short of leprosy should keep you from enjoying physical intimacy with at least one of the women in your life. And maybe more than one.

Now don't tell yourself as you read this that the reason you haven't had much sensual contact with the opposite sex of late is that you're just not getting enough encouragement from the women you go out with, because traditionally the female role is one of passive responsiveness. Whether that is due to biological factors or merely cultural ones is a matter of some dispute, but despite feminist rhetoric it's a fact of life that we all have to live with, for the time being at least. So don't be content to wait and hope, because you may be rationalizing an overblown fear of rejection and never escape from the rut you've fallen into if you do.

Now think about the last few relatively extended, solo encounters you've had with a woman. Did you:

1) Touch her cheek
2) Stroke her hair
3) Hold her hand
4) Hug her
5) Kiss her

If you've done all five recently you probably don't need to read this chapter. And if you've done only two or three, you're not doing bad. But if you're like a lot of the guys who phone me on radio and television call-in shows and whom I teach in my seminars, chances are that you could use some advice on how to improve your score.

Kirk, who participated in my seminar in Washington,

D.C., is just such a guy. At twenty-five he's reasonably good-looking and a successful law student, so he has the basic confidence to pull a lot of women into his orbit. But beyond that he gets stuck. "I don't know why my relationships with women are so blah," he lamented. "They just never seem to get off the ground. I can't even seem to get a good-night kiss!"

Kirk, this chapter is for you and for guys just like you, who, day after day, date after date, find themselves talking but not touching, hoping but not holding, being courteous but not kissing. Here are ten techniques for transforming your platonic relationships into the kinds of physical, sensual ones that all healthy males seek.

DON'T BE EMBARRASSED ABOUT YOUR DESIRES. Holding, hugging, touching, tasting, kissing, caressing—there are a zillion ways to make physical contact with a woman. And you, undoubtedly, would like to try every one of them. But something stops you.

What makes your hands freeze as you're about to touch a woman, your mouth tighten up as you're about to say something intimate and sexy? Probably it's just good old-fashioned guilt. Somewhere along the line you've gotten the idea that there's something wrong or barbaric in wanting what you want, even though you know it's what everybody wants—physical intimacy. So just as you're about to let your hand on its own natural impulse slide down the sleek back of the fair-haired creature sitting next to you, the image of your mother waving her finger at you the way she did when she once caught you reading *Playboy* comes hurtling into your mind. You sputter and pull your hand away, blush, and then, as if to change the subject, make some banal remark.

At the moment that you pulled your hand away you thought that there was something dirty about your desires, and that if the woman you were with knew about them she'd slap you in the face, pick up her bag, and walk away. But nothing, let me assure you, could be further from the truth. Women love to be touched—and a whole lot more. As a matter of fact, by some standards—such as orgasm potential—their need for physical contact is greater than our own. So when it comes to wanting physical (and sexual) intimacy, it is certainly not an us-against-them situation.

You should also remember that touching, holding, caressing, and so forth, are not in themselves necessarily sexual actions. They are merely indicators of warmth and tenderness, reflections of affection. Mothers touch children, friends touch friends, my nephew pets his dog. So there's really no need to get defensive about something that by and large does not necessarily carry any sexual connotation to it.

USE BODY LANGUAGE. As soon as you meet a woman, without any actual physical contact occurring, you can create the kind of ambience that leads to physical intimacy simply by the way you use and position your body. There's at least one whole book out on the subject, so I'll just give you a few basic pointers here.

Keep your body relaxed and open toward the woman with whom you are talking. Do not continuously keep your arms or your legs crossed, as this makes you look like a tight and unyielding person. Do not move either very close or very far away. Rather, pick a safe neutral distance, maybe a few feet, and gradually move closer. Find excuses to move closer, like getting her a drink or showing her something in a book.

Keep your movements soft and controlled rather than jerky and abrupt. The "dance" of physical seduction begins the moment you meet a woman. So at all times try to appear fluid and relaxed. That's the most important thing. If you seem sweaty and tense and itchy, it's unlikely that a whole lot of melting together is going to occur.

Related to this, of course, is the way you use your voice and eyes. Keep your voice pleasant and inviting, but firm and decided. It is like acne of the vocal chords to sound either wishy-washy or gruff. Since I talked about the importance of eye contact earlier, I won't dwell on it here. Just remember that the more of it, the better.

TEST HER WITH TOUCHING. As you're in a conversation with a woman, it's only natural for little bits of physical contact to occur. Your knee might slide against hers, she might touch you on the arm at a joke you made, or you might pat each other on the shoulder as you say good-bye. Try to make these contacts happen as often as possible, because meaningless as they may seem they are quite essential to building up the necessary trust and familiarity for grand-scale romance and sexual coupling later on.

Let me caution you not to expect too much from these little moments of physical contact. Some guys assume they've struck out if the woman they just touched on the cheek doesn't immediately demand sex. But the contrary is true: As long as she doesn't flinch you can congratulate yourself that things are going well.

There's a simple way to boost the speed with which casual touching can occur, and that is to openly express your physical attraction for a woman. Tell her what's on your mind, that she has a beautiful face, gorgeous hair, or perfect hands. Then touch the part of her you just praised, as if to see if something that beautiful can be real. As long as you don't start off by complimenting her genitalia, it's a perfectly smooth way to initiate a woman to the thrill of your delicate—and appreciative—touch.

BE PHYSICALLY SUPPORTIVE. Putting your arm around a woman if it's cold, taking her by the arm as you cross the street, helping her out of a cab—not only are these great excuses for making physical contact, but they will redound to your credit as acts of courtesy. Women regard men who take care of them in such a way as chivalrous and romantic.

I was talking about the importance of being physically supportive to women on a radio show one night when Bob, a salesman from Philadelphia, called in with a great anecdote. He and a date finished dinner at a fancy restaurant only to discover that it was pouring outside and the streets were flooded. Bob's date, in high heels, was afraid to walk outside of the sheltered area they were standing in. So Bob picked her up and carried her to his car across the street! As he opened the car door with her still in his arms he got a round of applause from the people standing under shelter. He returned home—with her—a hero.

BE IMAGINATIVE. Challenge her to a thumb wrestle, an arm wrestle, or an Indian wrestle. Show her the latest dance step you learned. Put a flower in her hair, your hat on her head, or your coat around her. The possibilities are unlimited.

My friend Roger told me the story of how he broke the ice with the girl he dated for most of his college years. He had gone out with her a few times, but each date had ended pretty dryly in front of her dorm with a "see ya in class." Then one day he ran into her down at the gym. "Care to learn a few wrestling moves?" he proposed. (Of course it helped that Roger had wrestled in high school.) At first she hesitated, but Roger cajoled her a bit and finally she accepted. After five minutes on the mat they had done more touching than most couples do on their honeymoon. And the physical intimacy stayed with them long after they had showered up. Roger told me that he didn't get the final pin until four in the morning.

TICKLE HER. Rob, a friend of mine who's a photographer, was sitting around one Wednesday night watching television with his girlfriend, Marie. Marie is a pretty Irish girl from Boston whose puritanical upbringing made it difficult for her to relax about any physical contact between them. So Rob came up with the perfect ploy. He tickled her. The spontaneity of the act and the laughter it evoked allowed them to pass the barriers they had been stuck at before. Tickling may seem like a childish thing to do, but, as Rob reported, the results can be most adult.

SHARE SENSUAL EXPERIENCES. Participate in the most extravagantly sensual experiences you can with a woman—a great meal, a movie with beautiful cinematography, a walk along the beach. The world is filled with sensual activities, and experiencing them will make you feel more sensuous, ultimately, about each other.

MASSAGE HER. Just step behind a female friend and put your strong hands on her tired shoulders, applying pressure with your thumbs. I assure you no person in her right mind would stop you from doing this to her—it feels too good. You might want to say casually, "You look a little tight here, Melissa," as you begin your therapeutic action, knowing that people are invariably tight in their shoulders. And who knows? Melissa might like to come over that evening to have her lower back done. Have some massage oil available for this; it can make even a rank amateur seem like a professional masseur.

DON'T ASK WIMPY QUESTIONS. Don't ask things like "May I kiss you good night?" Women really don't want to be put on the spot like that. In fact they hate it. In general it's very uncomfortable for a woman to be on a date with a guy who acts like a namby-pamby, waiting for her approval before he orders the wine or takes her hand on a walk. It comes off as pleading. And no relationship can be healthy in that context. So when it comes to hugs, kisses, and the like, don't think of yourself as a charity case. You're giving as much as getting.

KISS HER AT AN UNEXPECTED MOMENT. Cathy, her chestnut mane of hair flowing, just knocked a terrific backhand shot down the baseline to beat your opponents in a game of doubles tennis. She's excited about how well she played and is feeling very secure. Don't let the opportunity pass. Run over and give her a quick hug and a kiss. Those kinds of victory celebrations could make tennis your favorite racket. And hers too.

Let me conclude by emphasizing that becoming more physical in your relationships with women does not mean becoming more brutal. Arm tackles and headlocks make poor foreplay. The techniques suggested here allow you to engage in physical contact with a woman without making it a major issue in her mind. You are being forward, but in a very nonthreatening way. This is the key.

As you'll find, being more imaginatively aggressive in how you relate to them physically will actually exert less pressure on women than the conventional wait-and-see posture that may be keeping you feeling so unfulfilled right now. Because despite the rhetoric of certain factions of the women's lib movement and whatever your mama may have told you, it is pleasant for a woman to be skillfully drawn into physical contact with a man. Sure, you're being manipulative, but it's the kind of manipulation that all people secretly yearn for. Without it probably none of us would have ever been born.

18

Look Like a Lover

I'm going to discuss a special way to get a woman to incorporate you into her daydreams. What's *special* about this method is that it works on all lusty heterosexual women, not only specific personality types. Even more important, it's something that's easily achievable by almost all lusty heterosexual men, not just guys who are six feet two inches tall and drive Alfa Romeos. What is it? Why nothing more than to *look* like a great lover.

Look like a great lover? What do I do, wear a condom over my head? Don a Robert Redford mask?

None of the above. To look like a great lover one simply has to *be* a great lover. And before your testicles shrivel up in terror because you fear that you're not, or you snort with macho arrogance because you're confident that if you only got the chance more often you'd be one hell of a stud, ask yourself this: *Have I ever brought a woman to orgasm? Do I know how to be gentle in bed? Do I know how to talk to a woman while making love? Do I take my time?*

If you feel secure and knowledgeable in your answers to the above questions, then I doubt that you've even got this far into my book. For the truth is, you're *already* a great lover and probably have as many women as you want, or the one *great* woman who makes your life complete.

But if your answers to the above questions are vague and uncertain; if your recollection of what goes on under the sheets is confused with what goes on in a wrestling match; if every time you sleep with a woman you feel like you're being judged by harsh and critical eyes; then you've got a little bit of "work" ahead of you. But don't despair. In fact, don't even be the slightest bit depressed. Because the kind of work I'm talking about is fun, more fun than just about anything else I can think of.

Furthermore, once the work is over, you will never have trouble attracting lovely women again. In fact all you'll have to do from then on is walk into a party or a bar or an art gallery or a supermarket, and you'll suddenly find women drawn to you as if you were wearing some maddeningly aphrodisiacal cologne.

All that's important now is your acceptance that perhaps you could use a little practice—that maybe, just maybe, there's more to lovemaking than what you learned on the street corner from your best pal.

Love the One You're With

In my New York City course on how to succeed with women, one of the questions that comes up most often is this: "I'm going out with this girl who's okay, but I'd really like to find someone better. Should I keep going out with her?"

My answer is a resounding *yes*. I'm a great believer in the getting together of people, not the staying apart, in giving of yourself rather than holding back, in being involved with others instead of holding yourself aloof in the name of artificially high standards.

This is not to say you shouldn't pursue women other than your lady friend who's "just okay," women whom you perhaps will like better. But are the couple of hours every other week you spend with this current girlfriend really that great a deterrent to meeting new women? I think not. No, I think to cut yourself off from a lady with whom you share at least a little warmth and affection is a big mistake. To me it's an indication that you're choosing the road to reclusiveness, to narcissism, to retreat into yourself.

Try to take an overview. What is likely to happen if you choose not to go out with the girl about whom you feel lukewarm but instead wander through a maze of crowded, loveless singles bars? I've already given you my opinion of the likelihood of your being successful if you take that route. Chances are nine out of ten you'll return home to your place alone, drunk, depressed, and about twenty-five dollars poorer.

On the other hand, if you do go out with your available lady friend, you could end up spending a glorious evening in bed, practicing your technique, becoming a finer lover.

And don't give me that crap about leading her on. Men are always telling me, "I'm worried she's getting too hung up on me. What happens when I don't call her next week? She'll be so hurt." Hmm, could that be just a wee bit of projecting your feelings onto her?

No, the truth is, both you and she are adults now, well aware of the pleasures and heartaches that are a part of getting involved with others. Men and women supply one another with companionship and affection and sexual gratification . . . and also hurt and rejection. By the time we're in our mid-twenties we should all be well aware of that. It's not your job to go around shielding the universe from hurt. After all, is anyone doing that for you?

Now back to the bedroom. When you go to bed with her,

does your available lady friend reach orgasm? If not, you should see to it that she does. This is not a book on sexual technique, nor has writing about where and how people touch one another ever been my forte. I can, however, recommend several excellent books on the subject: *Making Love, The Joy of Sex, How to Make Love to a Man* (which, curiously, tells you a whole lot more about making love to a woman—perhaps because it's written by a woman), and finally a book published by my own Symphony Press, *How to Make Love to a Single Woman,* by Robert M. I realize it's a bit chauvinistic of me to tout one of my own publications, but having just reread the book for about the dozenth time, I honestly can't recall having ever come across writing that seems so sensitive to a woman's need for gentleness and tenderness.

Peruse one of the aforementioned books with your lady friend, then experiment with what you've read. Study her anatomy. Really get to know what a woman's body is like. (Remember, the more you know, the more confident you'll be when you're with a woman you prize more highly.) Find out how she likes to be touched. Have her kiss and massage and stroke you where you like it best. Because you're relaxed with this woman, you'll be less concerned about making a great impression. This is at the very heart of becoming a great lover. Now is the time to satisfy your curiosities, to take your time. This woman likes you. She wants to please, to be of service. She'll be only too delighted to answer all those questions you've been dying to know the answers to but have been too afraid to ask.

Over the years I've heard countless wonderfully erotic anecdotes from men who were lucky enough to have been seduced by an older woman while still in their teens. So well tutored were they that by the time they stepped out into the world as eligible young men, they had no problem winning women whatsoever. Their experience in bed glistened in their eye, reverberated in their voice, showed in their gait.

I liken the girlfriend you're not yet ready to jump off lover's leap for to the older seductress. In each case, though hardly overwhelmed by love, you have the perfect opportunity to learn and to experiment, to practice and to hone your skills in as warm and accepting an environment as you could ask for. In each case, you will walk away from your lover—if you do walk away—a more confident and attractive man.

In other words, don't look a gift horse in the mouth. Who better to practice on than the woman who is madly in love with you? One slight word of caution. While she's helping you achieve your sexual potential, you may very well be doing the same for her. After several weekends of the two of you exploding in bed together, she may suddenly start to loom much larger in your affections. But, then, what'd be so bad about that?

Clean but Casual

Several weeks ago I did a small survey on how a great lover should dress. Although the women I interviewed all varied on details, the overall thrust of their answers was surprisingly unified. They want their men clean, very clean. Several spoke of "that delicious just-stepped-out-of-the-shower freshness."

On the other hand, guys, they don't want you to dress too neatly and formally. Most of them spoke of liking turtle-necks, sweaters, and open-necked shirts as opposed to stiff-collar shirts and ties. They preferred sports jackets to suits. They chose khakis, jeans, and corduroys more often than formal slacks. One woman said, "When a man dresses in a casual, loose style I get the feeling he's going to be that way in bed. Soft, gentle. If he's all trussed up in a suit I worry that he's going to be too formal and businesslike in the sack."

To tell you the truth, my own bias has always been for nice but casual clothes. So I was delighted to hear that just about every woman I interviewed agreed with me. I don't, of course, want to tamper with your dressing style if you've got it down to an art and feel secure and confident in the way you step out of the house in the morning. On the other hand, if you've been searching for a "look," if you've always felt that somewhere out there there was a way to dress that was just right for you, then you might explore the world of casual, tweedy, woodsy clothes. They're comfortable, reasonably priced, and women say they get turned on by men who wear them. What more could you ask?

I realize, of course, that if your interest has been piqued, you could probably use far more specific information on exactly what kind of pants, shoes, sweaters, and jackets to look for, in which case I'll recommend two books—*Looking Good* and *Dressing Right*—and *Gentleman's Quarterly* magazine. You might also send for catalogs from Brooks Brothers, Paul Stuart, and L. L. Bean. These companies all sell high-quality handsome clothing.

Let's conclude this chapter with a little review. The best way to look like a great lover is, above all, to *be* a great lover. The way you do that is by practicing. If you can't find a girl you love to practice with, then love the one you're with. And read one of the great recommended sex manuals to expand your knowledge and talents. Then, after you've mastered the art, walk out into the world and turn your newly confident lover's gaze onto any pretty lady who catches your fancy. She'll tingle all over under your piercing eyes, particularly if you look clean and casual. This not only communicates to a woman that you'll smell good in bed, but it also says that, rather than being uptight and rigid, you'll be gentle and soft and easygoing and all those other things that bring out the most passionate side of her nature. *Hallelujah!*

19

How to Get Women to Fantasize About You

Here is another way to inject a note of amorousness into any relationship you have with a woman that has got off on far too much of a platonic footing for your liking. Get her to fantasize about you.

Fantasize about me? may come your disbelieving rejoinder. *How the hell am I going to do that? I'm five feet seven and a half inches tall, ten pounds overweight, and losing my hair.*

Don't worry about it. You don't have to look like Nick Nolte or John Travolta to get women to fantasize about you. In fact that's one of the most wonderful things of all about women. Their fantasy lives are set in motion by such unpredictable and unexpected imagery that it'll make your head spin. But more than that, it'll make your heart pound with optimism and hope. For as you will see, getting a woman to fantasize about you has very little to do with what you look like at all—it is almost completely dependent on how a woman thinks and feels about herself. The real art in getting a woman to have sexy thoughts about you is in deciphering her personality, getting inside her head and psyche, figuring out exactly what it is that will trigger a sexy daydream, and, most important of all, making yourself the hero of said daydream. And I think you'll find that the following paragraphs offer some provocative and effective techniques for making it happen.

FEED HER SENSE OF EXHIBITIONISM. One of the things that makes a woman feel sexiest of all is to show herself to a man or a group of men. It doesn't matter whether the men are attractive or not. The unleashing of her erotic feelings seems to have totally to do with the act of displaying herself, of having others devour the most sacred parts of her flesh with their eyes and their imaginations, not with who is actually doing the devouring.

Think about it. The wife of a prestigious senator attends a state dinner at the White House in a black dress cut down to her naval. The senator himself wears a dull tuxedo.

A cheerleader leaps in the air displaying her behind and the very tops of her thighs to over one hundred thousand people, and if on national TV an additional 20 or 30 million. Do male cheerleaders do the same? Of course not. They leap into the air all right, but instead of tiny little panties they wear baggy, unrevealing trousers.

In our society, as in most societies, females spend a great deal of time, effort, ingenuity, and money in devising ways to provoke the opposite sex to look down their blouses and up their skirts. Males don't do the equivalent. Women libbers would have us believe that this is cultural, that we have been brainwashed into behaving so. Other people maintain that such behavior is biological and evolutionary, that it was genetically programmed into the two sexes millions of years ago.

I'm not sure what the origin is, but I do know that there is an important implication here. Women become sexually excited by both the reality and the fantasy of exhibiting themselves. And if you need further proof, just take a quick read through Nancy Friday's excellent book, *My Secret Garden*. Here women describe daydreams in which they are being watched by as few as one small grade-school lad to as many as an arena full of men. In these fantasies the women see themselves stripping, dancing, screwing, masturbating, undulating, you name it.

Would you have the same fantasy? I doubt it. Perhaps it's narrow-minded of me to claim it, but in all my years of researching and writing about men and women I've never once heard any man say he felt even the tiniest spark of excitement over the idea of parading naked in front of women. To exhibit ourselves simply does not seem to be a part of the collective masculine unconscious.

Okay, maybe you're thinking, *so women like to walk around in skimpy bikinis. Any fool who's ever been to Jones Beach can tell you that. What does that have to do with getting them to have prurient daydreams about me?*

Plenty. Put this knowledge to work for you. Indulge their need to be looked at. Ogle them. How about this woman you've been taking out for a month of weekends in a row, without touching, kissing, or doing any of those other things one does with a woman that feel so good? Let me ask you something. Does she wear tight pants? Low-cut blouses? Body-hugging dresses? Skirts with high slits up the side? If so, I suspect she's one of those women whose fantasies involve lots of self-display. So give her a hand. Instead of trying *not* to stare down her blouse, stare down her blouse aplenty. When she uncrosses and crosses her legs in front of you, direct your glance as far up her thighs as possible, boldly, unabashedly, rather than politely looking away. She, of course, would probably never admit that this is what she wants you to do. But you can be certain that if she is wearing revealing clothes, this is precisely what she does want you to do. And there is probably no better way to get her thinking about you sexually, both in daydream and real life, than by giving her what she wants—the very attention that she is so explicitly seeking out with her dress.

Out of the hundreds of women's exhibitionist fantasies I've come across over the years, I can hardly ever recall one in which the fantasizer described the man or men who were watching her. Almost always they were nameless, faceless souls. My interpretation of this is that the erotic feelings of the dreamer come exclusively from being watched, not from fantasizing who is watching her. Thus if you feel that you are not good-looking or sexy enough for the woman you are dating, and that this is why she is not reaching out to you sexually, forget it. Your appearance, assuming you are neat and clean and reasonably presentable, is relatively unimportant. The woman with exhibitionistic fantasies is far more interested in how she appears to you than how you appear to her.

My conclusion? If you are dating or pursuing or just being friendly with a woman who dresses revealingly, a woman whom you'd like to become involved with sexually, make an overt effort (I'm sure it really won't take much effort) to feast your eyes on her breasts, her haunches, her lips, and so forth. Do so brazenly, shamelessly. You may not notice results right away. But here's what is going to happen behind the scenes. One morning soon, while she's luxuriating in bed for a few minutes before she gets ready for work, she's going to lapse into one of her favorite exhibitionistic fantasies. While she searches about for a man to cast in her daydream, the chances are good that sooner or later she's going to settle on you. After all, you've indicated with your bold stare what an excellent candidate you are. And the more boldly and frequently you stare at her in real life, the more likely you are to turn up in her fantasy life. Why? Because you've tuned in to her. You're giving her the kind of erotic attention that excites her type of personality. And of course you don't have to be a genius to predict that once you're making appearances in her fantasy life, it won't be long before you begin popping up in her bed. For real.

BE A BROTHER TO HER. *But that's precisely the problem I'm having. We're like brother and sister together. Good pals but no nooky.*

My contention here is that if she's treating you like her brother, you may be a whole lot closer to sexual relations with her than you think, particularly if she has a brother in real life. My reasoning: Many a woman is obsessed with her brother. She probably won't admit it to you—unless, perhaps, you get extraordinarily close, marry her, and psychoanalyze her, and even then she may not fess up—but she may have the most wildly incestuous fantasies about her brother. In *My Secret Garden* one woman describes a lifelong fantasy that comes to mind every time she has intercourse with her husband. She imagines that her husband is her younger brother and that her older brother is standing over them, watching. When the younger brother reaches orgasm, he shifts places with the older brother and the scene is reenacted. The woman who has this fantasy says it never fails to electrify her with the most erotic of feelings. Yet she sounds, from her choice of language and writing style, like a perfectly sane, literate, thoughtful person. Another woman in *My Secret Garden* writes that she fills her fantasy life with enormous, lusty family orgies. Yet another states, "To make a man sexy to myself, I just imagine him a member of my family."

Let this be an inspiration to you.

Does the woman you're pursuing have a brother. If you don't know, ask her. If it turns out she does, get her to talk about him. Watch how a look of pride and happiness begins to pervade the air. Now how do you take advantage of all this?

It's easy. Treat her like a sister. Be a pal, the way a

brother might, even going so far as to call her Sis. If her brother is older, kid her like an older brother would. If she's got a younger brother, act a little helpless, as a kid brother might. But whatever you do, keep it brotherly. Try to think of the two of you as siblings. Tell her you really feel comfortable around her, like she's your sister or something. And don't push things or try to speed them up. For here's what's going to be happening in her mind. She's going to pick up on your brotherly vibes and start to feel the same kind of affection for you that she feels for her own brother. It's going to make her feel very relaxed, very happy, very at peace with you, just like she does with her own brother. The only difference, of course, is that you're not her brother. And so she's going to be able to do something with you that she can't in good conscience do with her real brother, no matter how strong her desire.

But again, take your time. Let the brotherly quality of your relationship establish itself and flourish. Call her for just a chat. Have lunch with her to find out how she's doing. Joke about the brother-sister nature of your relationship. Before long she'll probably be having the hottest fantasies about you she's ever had about anyone. Then, when you feel the aura of "family" has really taken hold, drop by her place with a couple of bottles of wine. Get good and high together. Then make your play. At first she may be horrified. How could you, someone who's been so brotherly to her? But the temptation will be too strong. Deep in her heart, this is what she's really wanted since she's reached puberty. And the alcohol and the fact that you're not really her brother after all will be the clinchers. The actual lovemaking will be heavenly, mind-blowing, because the whole experience will be tinged with the hint of incest, of the forbidden, which often adds such a kicker to sex.

ACT WITH AUTHORITY. A surprising number of women like to be dominated in some way, or at least like to fantasize about being dominated in some way. And it's up to you to act the role of potential dominator.

Up to me? you gasp. *But I can't even get my little sister to fix me a sandwich. Trained animals refuse to obey me in simple commands. How am I going to*—you shudder—*dominate somebody I hardly know, somebody I've been trying so hard just to be nice to?*

Relax. All I'm suggesting is that you allow yourself to reveal a dominating side to your personality, and this isn't quite as stark a proposition as it first might sound. First of all, you have to be honest with yourself. What the hell, wouldn't you like to tell people what to do and have them do it. Wouldn't you like to say, "C'mon, Julia, give me a kiss," and have Julia immediately melt her mouth into yours? All right then, so there is a potentially dominating side to your personality.

Second, and even more important, you have to recognize that many people, beautiful women included, yearn to be told what to do. At first this may seem a little hard to believe, but it really isn't when you stop to think about it. The reason lies in the complexity of human psychology, especially as it regards matters of mystery and taboo, like sex. Because women are brought up for the most part to see sex as something dangerous and forbidden, they need a way to relieve the guilt attending it. Not being in control is the simplest way for them to achieve this.

Now remember, all we're after at this point is to make you a sexually charged object in a woman's mind. So I'm not suggesting that you tie your date up in your Volkswagen on your way to the movies. What I am suggesting is that you reveal the kind of strong, forceful, and determined personality that a woman will intuitively realize can lead her to the kind of places that she secretly wants to go. Like to bed. With you.

But you ask, *How can I reveal this personality without taking the risk of permanently offending a potential lover?* That's easy; go slowly. The transition I'm talking about is really a very subtle one. Instead of asking in a nasal voice, "Would you maybe like to have dinner together sometime next week?" boom out, "Hey, I'm starving to death, and I know a great little Italian restaurant. Let's go!" As you whisk her into your car she'll be too exhilarated to wonder whether proper decorum has been followed.

If you need further food for thought upon this matter, let me refer you to Sigmund Freud's now generally accepted hypothesis that a child's first sexual interest centers upon the parent of the opposite sex. For women this means the father, and what greater authority figure is there? Women, according to Freudian theory, spend their entire lives searching for a man whom they can obey as they once did their father, a man whose authority is unquestionable, and who can therefore "legitimize" their sex lives. This man might as well be you.

If you're convinced by now (and you should be) that exhibiting an authoritative personality occasionally is a good way to make women fantasize about you sexually and romantically, then it's up to you to play the part. Don't be afraid to build up your biceps a bit and wear boots, as well as work on your voice intonation. I would suggest that you stop somewhere short of carrying a machete, however, unless you're really after hard-core types.

TAKE HER TO EXOTIC, EROTIC SETTINGS. Many female fantasies have nothing to do with a particular man or type of man but focus, rather, on a certain type of setting or environment. The demure blonde sitting next to you on the bus may go home every night and dream of having love made to her while she floats down the Amazon on a raft. The proximity of crocodiles turns her on. Or your cute lab partner may dwell regularly on how great sex would be in a swimming pool. She has a new type of breast stroke in mind. Some of these fantasies are obviously impossible to actualize, and some are quite feasible. Unfortunately, in most cases there is little way for you to find out what a woman's fantasies are regarding a setting or environment for love-making.

Well, Eric, you say, a bit miffed, *why'd you bring the subject up in the first place then? Your book is supposed to encourage me. When it comes to love and sex I don't need to spend money to read about negatives.*

Have faith! Would I present a cloud unless there was a silver lining? And the silver lining is this: While you may not be able to pinpoint a woman's exact fantasy place or setting, chances are you'll be able to come up with a few of your own that are pretty exciting to most women. Like Paris.

Now before you start screaming that I'm bonkers, hear me out. I'm not proposing that you actually take a date to Paris for the weekend (although if you could pull it off it would be great). I'm suggesting that you merely get yourself *associated* with a romantic place like Paris in a woman's mind. And this isn't as hard to achieve as you might think.

The truth of the matter is, my friend, that you can be just as Parisian as you want to be, right there in Peoria, Illinois, or wherever you happen to be. No, this does not entail feigning a French accent or being pretentious in any way. (But you might want to try feigning a French accent sometime just for the experience.) All you have to do is as follows: Dress yourself in European-cut clothing and wear a French cologne (be understated); take your date to a warm and romantic French film, such as *Cousin, Cousine,* if you can find one playing in town; and follow that up by going to the best and most intimate French restaurant in your area. By the end of the evening your date will be thinking that there is something very unique and alluring about French culture, even if it has never occurred to her before. And you'll be the man she primarily associates with that culture.

I guarantee it—you won't have to take your date to

France to make this work. Within a week or two she'll be dreaming about your saying, *"Voulez-vous . . ."*

There are any number of variations on this. How about a Polynesian restaurant followed by a walk on the beach. Tropical settings are very erotic for many women, what with the sound of waves, cool breezes, and so on. Amid all these primal associations you will be Man, the provider. What better fantasy image could you want? Before long your Woman will be pulling you both down behind the sand dunes for some primal fun.

Space does not allow the decoding here of the many other types of female fantasies. But I do have two suggestions for you. One, that you get a hold of Nancy Friday's *My Secret Garden* and do a little decoding yourself. And two, that you listen very, very carefully to the women to whom you're attracted. If you do, you're going to discover the hidden keys to their interior fantasy life.

The severe dresser in the office next to you may have dominance fantasies and may start to show real interest in you if she gets a sense you'd enjoy being tied to her bed. The girl sitting next to you in biology, who is always talking about her father, may spark to your taking a stern, grown-up air with her.

The world is full of possibilities, and if you watch and listen closely enough, you're going to be rewarded richly. *Vive la fantaisie.*

20

Creative Courtship

You can go out on a lot of great dates with a woman, but for a relationship to get really intense, really exciting, something more is needed. And that something is continuity.

After all, even if you flew a gal to Paris on a Saturday night for dinner at Maxim's (one of the fanciest restaurants in the world), chances are that by Wednesday, if not Tuesday or even Monday, her mind would be back on other subjects besides you—her work, new curtains for her apartment, or, most excruciating of all, other men. The spell of an evening, no matter how perfect that evening was, cannot last forever.

So you want to find other ways besides dates to integrate yourself into a woman's life, to become as meaningful to her on Tuesday morning as you are on Saturday night, to be not simply a good date but part of her life. And achieving this meaningfulness is what this chapter is designed to help you do by opening your eyes to unique possibilities for courtship.

Throughout history, courtship has been a highly intricate art form. Unfortunately, in our time most men have lost the sense of it. Oh sure, a guy will send flowers once in a while, and that alone will make a woman's face light up with joy. But there are so many more unique and diverse courting opportunities in our society. Unfortunately, most men don't have the imagination to take advantage of them.

Don't be one of this sad majority. If you've been staying away from courting because you think it means putting on armor and climbing into castles (which is not exactly your style) or throwing your coat over puddles to keep women from getting their feet wet (which would make your dry-cleaning bills too high), I've got good news for you. The kind of courtship I'm talking about has nothing to do with those antiquated activities. As you're about to see, my courting techniques are simple, inexpensive, and a lot of fun to practice. As you read on, you'll probably come up with some more ideas of your own, but here are seven great ones to get you started—and to keep you going—on this most important aspect of winning with women.

SEND HER A NOTE. A note is basically just a few words written down on a piece of paper. You may have stopped passing them in the fourth grade, when old Miss Dingleberry threatened to send you to the principal's office if you didn't. But now is a good time to take the practice up again. Why? Because a woman loves to get a message meant only for her. Even if that message is no more exotic than a recipe for banana cake, the idea itself is unique and romantic. It establishes an intimacy between the sender and sendee.

When you send a message in a note, you can get away with something that's a lot wilder and more risqué than what you could say directly. "Miss Wilson, you look absolutely gorgeous today." Sending notes is a great way to communicate, and just having the idea and the gumption to do it will make you stand out.

Sending notes, by the way, can also be a great way to pick women up. Try it in a bar, a restaurant, on a plane, at a party, anywhere. Aaron, a college student, had the idea to do it one night at an all-night diner. He was completely enamored with his waitress but couldn't build up the courage to say anything more daring than "May I have another cup of coffee?" So he wrote on a napkin: "You are too beautiful for words. May I please buy you lunch tomorrow at twelve-thirty at the Waldorf?" Guess what? Aaron showed up and so did she! And they've been seeing each other ever since.

SEND HER A LETTER. I'm making this a separate suggestion from the above one because a letter is a lot longer than a note and, as you're about to see, can have a quite different effect.

The basic difference between a letter and a note is the degree of formality. A letter is usually longer and more carefully written. It is something that a woman thinks about keeping and rereading for the rest of her life. So when you send a woman a letter, it can be a part of you that she'll never let go, a gift, really, that she'll always treasure. For this reason letters used to be a very common technique of courtship.

Even though you were probably brought up with a telephone in your room and the only letter you've ever written was the one in summer camp that your counselor made you write to your parents, there's no reason not to pick up the old quill now and give it a try. Who knows what you may come up with?

But if you're really insecure about your powers of written communication, I have one very useful suggestion. Keep your own writing short and make the body of the letter a poem that you like. Now I know that some of you may think that this is a very corny idea, but try to view it this way: Poetry is written romance, and women, as I've emphasized over and over again, love romance. And it's all just sitting there, millions of pages of poetry, waiting to be used by you.

If you are a good writer you may not want to include a whole poem. How about just the first two lines of Shakespeare's most famous sonnet?

> Shall I compare thee to a summer's day?
> Thou art more lovely and more temperate.

Now what woman wouldn't want to read that addressed to her? Shakespeare wrote over a hundred sonnets, many of which you could appropriate for your own purposes. Or, if you don't like him, just check out any anthology of love poetry. You'll find thousands of poems to choose from, from the hauntingly surreal to the knee-slappingly funny, one to delight and surprise every woman you know.

A variation on this, if you want to be more contemporary, is to copy down the lyric of a romantic rock ballad and send that. There are a lot of rock lyrics that work quite well as written poetry—stuff by the Beatles, Dave Mason, Jesse Colin Young, to name just a few of the artists whose work you might consider.

I'm sure you've sung songs with a particular girl in mind. Well, what the hell, let yourself go and let the girl know that a song reminds you of her. She'll be as moved by the eloquence of the words as if they were your own.

PUT A MESSAGE IN THE CLASSIFIEDS. There are many paths to the heart, but one of the best is through the ego. Seeing a message in print meant just for them is pretty exciting for most people, a way of having their specialness flaunted to the world.

The more personal and the more it sets the two of you off against the world, the better. What's great about this is that it's likely to be a unique experience in a woman's life. Almost all of us read the personals, but how many of us actually get in there? It will be a message she'll always remember.

By the way, you can actually run personal ads on the front page of many of the nation's largest newspapers, including the New York *Times.*

SHOW HER YOUR BABY PICTURES. We all look cute as kids, so why not let her have that perspective on you? Seeing baby pictures of a guy is something that a lot of women told me they really enjoy. So break out the old photo album the next time you have a woman over to your place. Seeing those sweet shots of you will make her want to cuddle and hug you all night. Home films, despite the bad rep they have, are something that a lot of women told me they would enjoy seeing as well. They feel privileged to be let in on all those tender moments of your past that the camera has recorded. There's something about seeing the child a man once was that many women consider erotic.

DO SOMETHING UNUSUAL ON YOUR LUNCH BREAK. How about treating her to a sauna in a health club, going for a horse and buggy ride, or finding a place to go dancing? Don't be afraid to extend the hour a little bit to make it something that will really alter the complexion of a day, a day that otherwise would be all too similar to the days around it.

One especially good activity you can ask a female friend to do during lunch hour is to help you choose a gift for your mother, aunt, sister, old high-school teacher, or friend who's getting married. Shopping together breeds intimacy, so it's excellent strategy for a relationship that's just getting off the ground. And any woman will be flattered that you seek out her opinions and judgment on something as personal as choosing a gift for someone you care about.

INCLUDE HER YOUNGER SIBLING ON AN OUTING. Or include her niece, nephew, cousin, or even the little kid next door to her, if she doesn't have a brother or sister. Find out about her family situation, because it will convey to a woman that you care about her.

In fact one woman I interviewed, Clara, told me that the attentiveness a man paid to her little brother convinced her, ultimately, to marry that man. "Jerry and I had been going out on and off for about two months, but I really didn't see the potential for a truly significant relationship," she told me. "Then one Saturday he came over to take me to the beach. While I went upstairs to change into my bathing suit, he started talking to my little brother, Frankie. When I came downstairs Jerry announced a new plan: We were taking Frankie to the circus.

"At first it surprised me, but then I was impressed. I thought to myself, *How many guys would want to spend their Saturday taking a kid to the circus?* We had a great day together. By the end of it I knew that Jerry was someone special; Frankie and he got along so well. When I finally did decide to marry Jerry, this was a big factor."

Fellas, you may not be looking to get married, but you do want women to feel like they might want to marry you. So pay attention to their families, especially any younger brothers or sisters. A trip to the circus or the zoo may pay bigger dividends than a fancy, formal, and expensive date.

SHOOT A ROLL OF FILM ON HER. "Linda, you look so great today," you say. "Mind if I take your picture?" Linda may act nonchalant or even protest slightly, but actually she'll be delighted. Asking if you can take her picture is a subtle way of complimenting a woman on her beauty.

If you really want a way to make your "model" feel good, get "carried away" and shoot a whole roll of film on her. "How about one on the front porch," you say. "The light's interesting over there." After that: "Could I take one with your hair down—you look completely different that way." Just keep snapping away, being creative, looking for the most flattering settings and angles. It will be a delightful experience for both you and her, playing photographer and model. And who knows, it may lead the two of you into the realm of the erotic.

If you've shot a whole roll on her, at least one shot is more than likely to come out well. Of course you should give her a copy, but for a surprise she'll really get off on, have it blown up into poster size. I bet she's never been given a gift like that—to be suddenly made into a poster girl. Hang it up on her bedroom wall. And include a note: "Farrah Fawcett, watch out!"

21

Wooing a Woman with Gifts

Much of this chapter grows out of seminars I conduct in New York City and elsewhere for men who want to improve their love lives. I frequently lead off these seminars by asking how many of the participants keep a savings account.

I ask that question because I find that there is a striking correlation between being concerned with saving money and *not* succeeding with women. And indeed I almost invariably see a strong show of hands among the students in these seminars. In fact I would say I almost invariably see a *proud* show of hands. It's as if these guys think that having a savings account makes them superior citizens, better husband prospects, and generally more mature. And who am I to say that they are wrong?

But, and perhaps unfortunately, the guy who tries to save every extra dime he can is usually not the guy saddled with a pleasantly burdensome social life, not the guy with two blondes draped around each shoulder and a black book stuffed with more numbers than the Manhattan telephone directory. No, more often than not, the chap who continually puts away for a rainy day is the chap who spends a lot of sunny Saturdays by himself, and this is one of the important facts I try to bring out in my seminars. Certainly money is not the source of a good relationship, but, like it or not, money can often act as a social lubricant, a catalyst, to bring intimacy and excitement into the interactions that men and women have with each other.

It's part pride and part frugality, but a lot of guys won't accept this fact as pertaining to them. They think, *Hey, women should love me for who I am—they should love me if I don't spend a dime on them.*

Well, I'm sorry to say that the world does not operate within such idealistic, nonmaterialistic boundaries. Women don't walk down the street being able to read the souls of all the men they encounter. They aren't able to make transcendent leaps into interpersonal awareness any more than you can. They need cues and positive indicators. So if you're a nice guy, one worth their while to know and ultimately care for, you've got to find ways to convey this. And the act of spending money on a woman, as I've mentioned in earlier chapters, tends to be a great conveyer.

Now don't get alarmed as you read this. I am not advocating the wholesale expenditure of your life's savings to finance your love life. If you have to sell your car to buy a ring for a girl—even the girl you love—don't do it. If you have to give up eating for a week to pay for one extravagant dinner, don't do it. Because no woman in her right mind (the only kind you should be interested in) would want a man to go into the poorhouse for her. What women do respond to—and I've had them tell me this over and over again—is a spirit of generosity, of giving because you care, of not holding back when it is within your means to do something nice.

So if you started reading "Wooing a Woman with Gifts"

somewhat apprehensively, afraid that it would center mostly around yachts and diamonds, you're in for a pleasant surprise. I'm not asking you to deck out all the women you know like Nancy Reagan on a formal occasion, or even like Elizabeth Taylor on an informal occasion. No, I've got some gift ideas that may well cost you less than this book did and that will probably be almost as good an investment. Gift ideas that will make you stand out as having a warm, generous, and even artistic spirit and that could make your presence felt in a woman's life for years to come.

A COPY OF YOUR FAVORITE BOOK OR ALBUM. A gift that tells a woman something about you can have a very powerful effect, drawing her nearer to you without your actually being there. If you appreciate literature or music, the work that you most enjoy or closely relate to is a great way of conveying to a woman the kind of person you are, or at least conveying to her one intriguing, dynamic aspect of yourself.

A friend of mine who's a writer has given a copy of the play *Hamlet* to several of the women he's gone out with. "I've read the play dozens of times myself, so I enjoy having the opportunity to give my interpretation of it," he told me. "And most of my girlfriends find the play quite exciting when I've explained it to them. But how I really score points is by telling them how strongly I relate to the main character, how my trials and tribulations and existential woes are so much like Hamlet's. This usually fills them with a deep sympathy for me, which, naturally, I make the most of."

The book you give out, of course, does not need to be *Hamlet* or anything nearly as literary. The important thing is to make it one that you like and that you think the woman you give it to will like. That way you can be drawn closer to each other through it. The idea is to make it an active and shared element of your lives.

If either you or your girlfriend is not exactly into reading, a musical album is probably a better gift. If the Beach Boys are your favorite group of all time, give her their best album. Or you might want to give her something soft and perhaps even classical. Either way, try to make it a unique component of her collection. That way she's more likely to think of you whenever she plays it.

A CAKE YOU BAKED. Or make her a quiche, or any kind of unusual and good-tasting homemade food item.

The stomach, as the old adage goes, is one of the best ways to the heart, and if you have some skill in the kitchen there is nothing wrong with a little role reversal. As a matter of fact, given the predominance of feminist attitudes among most women today, showing that you not only have some skills in the kitchen but don't mind using them is probably one of the best ways to enhance your image. What's more, you'll probably get some good food in return.

Food, by the way, is one of the most traditional of all gifts, though it's availability in our society has tended to reduce its usage in that role. Nonetheless, you can't help liking someone who gives you something good to eat. If you can't cook yourself, you might look into having a cake or other baked item especially made up. It will be remembered long after it's consumed.

A HOMEMADE PIECE OF FURNITURE. Chances are that you may have more skill in carpentry than you do in the kitchen, and if that is the case you should saw and nail your homemade gift rather than mix and bake it. This takes some work, but it's a way to come up with a beautiful and enduring present for a relatively small amount of money. Just try and keep your creations on the pretty and delicate side . . . a small jewelry box, perhaps, or a framed mirror.

If you have a different hobby—say, pottery, photography, or even poetry—don't keep it an unknown part of your life. Take advantage of the skills you've developed to create gifts from them. Numerous women have told me that a gift that someone makes himself has a lot more impact than one bought in a store.

A SEXY DRESS. This is one of those great gifts that you both benefit from. While she gets to look sexy, you get to look at her look sexy. Buying attractive clothes can run you into a few more bucks, but the results are well worth it. It's the kind of gift that not only can stimulate fun-filled evenings, it can change the whole complexion of a relationship. Most women are somewhat shy about dressing sexy, and therefore feeling sexy. They need encouragement in that direction. So *encourage!*

FLOWERS. Look, I know I'm always stressing the importance of being original, but some clichés are just such good ideas that they need to be suggested anyway. Men have been giving flowers to women for centuries, and for centuries women have been responding with delight. As Debbie, a pretty, curly-haired nurse, told me, "If a guy wants to make me feel tender and romantic toward him, all he has to do is give me flowers. That automatically makes him jump up about ten notches on my list of favorite men."

I'm not sure why flowers have such a potent effect, but I think it has something to do with beauty for the sake of beauty. Although the women I interviewed were divided on the question of whether a gift should be practical, I got the feeling that most of them actually preferred gifts that weren't. And flowers epitomize this quality in a gift. Of course, diamonds do, too. But who can afford diamonds?

A POSTER OF THE TWO OF YOU. Have a photo of the two of you blown up into poster size. The effect? Dramatic. Your relationship will seem larger than life.

A TEAPOT. Did you know that there are some quite beautiful and exotic teapots from the Far East that can be bought for well under ten dollars? When you give this gift include a package of teas. Every time a cup is brewed in the pot you'll be thought of.

I'm not a big tea drinker myself. I got this idea from Yvonne, a sophisticated, dark-haired divorcée, who told me about the teapot that Jim, a man she went out with several years ago, gave her.

"I haven't seen Jim in an awfully long time, but do you know I think of him almost every day! Every morning, to be more precise, over my morning cup of tea. And the teapot itself is so beautiful it stands out as a kind of central object in my kitchen. Of all the gifts I've ever received it's one of the most enduring."

A CONTINUAL BARRAGE OF SMALL GIFTS. Anytime you give a gift you've done something special, no matter how tiny, inexpensive, or insignificant the gift may seem to you. A small bottle of perfume, a bead necklace, a T-shirt with some special message on it, even just a cupcake or a brownie—receiving any one of these can make a woman far happier than the monetary value of the item itself would indicate. What's important, what's registering in the mind of the woman whom you're favoring with gifts, is that a relationship is being established which is one of warm and affectionate generosity. Because being able to give to someone, as Erich Fromm discusses in his excellent book *The Art of Loving,* is the essence of being able to love someone. That's why an exchange of gifts can be a truly important factor in a developing relationship and why even small gifts can make a woman think big of you. They're one of the most positive indicators she can have about your ultimate capacity as a lover.

22

Sinking Your Teeth In

Congratulations! You're involved with a woman. You may not be married yet, you may not be even going steady, but you and she have clicked. You're seeing each other more than casually, more than incidentally. She's a part of your life. Now, how can you keep her that way?

First of all, don't get nervous about the situation, even if this is the first time that you're involved in something this big. Keep on doing what you've been doing—acting relaxed, being nice, enjoying the time you and she spend together. That's not a bad formula for success. After all, it's taken you this far.

But that doesn't mean you can just coast. Relationships don't maintain themselves magically. In fact if a relationship is not changing, growing, and expanding, it's actually deteriorating. There's no such thing as one just standing still. That's called stagnation.

Now is a good time to put even more energy into the

relationship. There are some things you can do to make it really take off, to make her think of you as even more special than she already does. You've planted the seed, now make it sprout. The following twelve techniques, which I've purposefully saved for the last chapter of the book, are designed to win you the greatest of all possible gifts on earth—a woman's love.

TAKE HER ON A VACATION. No matter how great your relationship might seem in Moffetville, Wyoming, chances are that an exotic environment would make it seem even better.

There is no better project to blow some bucks on!

If you have very minimal bucks to blow, make it a more or less local vacation—a camping trip, a weekend at a luxurious hotel in a major city, a drive into a neighboring county where there's a state fair, a music festival, or some other interesting event. I'd love to give you more specific suggestions, but it all depends, of course, on what part of the country (or world) you happen to be living in.

I suspect that the majority of my readers, however, could afford something a little bit more extravagant than a local trip if they felt they could justify the expenditure. And I'm telling you right now, it is justified. A vacation together for two lovers is one of the greatest experiences possible—a memory that will always, always be a source of delight and inspiration. Don't hesitate.

Where are the best places to go? The top few that stand out in my mind, from personal experience, are the South of France, the Caribbean, and the English countryside, and I have a strong love for the Oregon coast. Talk to your travel agent for more ideas and to find out the best fares available. There are some incredibly cheap fares to Europe especially. The time of your life could cost you less than a visit to the dentist.

FIX HER FAUCETS. No, I'm not talking metaphorically here. I mean, if you have any handyman skills, put them to use for her. Give her car a tune-up, or give her bedroom a new coat of paint, or tighten the washers on her dryer. This is one very tangible way to make her feel you can make her life better.

If you don't have those kinds of skills, help her out in other ways. Feed her cat if she's away for a day, help her fill out her tax return, show her the best way to defrost her fridge. *Helping* her is an important way of *loving* her.

ASK HER IF SHE HAS ANY SEXUAL FANTASIES THAT YOU COULD HELP HER FULFILL. Do this in a subtle, supporting way, so as not to make her feel on the spot. But then don't be embarrassed yourself if she asks you to put a mirror on her ceiling, cover her body with whipped cream, or call her dirty names. You never know what somebody thinks of as a turn-on.

The benefit of this is that it can lead to some absolutely earth-shaking, soul-satisfying sex—a benefit, obviously, you both share in. And you'll probably end up having some of your secret fantasies fulfilled, too.

Sex is an area that it is somewhat difficult to communicate about, because of all the taboos surrounding it. I urge you to break down the barriers as soon as you can, force yourself to, even if it means a red face and a lump in your throat, because very few relationships survive without a healthy dose of lust satiation. So get down and get dirty with one another. And if you get a bit too dirty, follow it up with the next idea.

TAKE A BUBBLE BATH TOGETHER. Need I give any explanation? This is a fun time that can be engineered almost instantaneously. Just take the initiative to get the bath ready sometime. You'll come out feeling more than clean.

TAKE HER SHOPPING. I've made this suggestion in other contexts, but I'll repeat it because it's a traditional favorite among women. They love pretty things, and choosing one or two among many gives them a thrill that men seldom experience (except with cars and prostitutes).

What can you take women shopping for? Dishes, books, jewelry—but above all, clothes. And when you buy a woman something to wear that makes her look pretty and feels comfortable, you're doing both of you a favor.

TREAT HER LIKE A FRIEND. Eighty percent of being compatible lovers is being good friends, which means, really, just unselfconsciously enjoying the time you spend together. This takes a while to achieve, because it is a function of developing a shared sensibility, an intuitive understanding of what you'll both enjoy together—the kind of thing you may have had with your best buddy from high school or college.

So think of your best few relationships with males, and try to apply what made those good to your relationship with the woman (or women) who is right now making your life special—the sense of adventurousness, of mutual support, of pride in each other. That, being the essence of friendship, is also the essence of love.

DON'T TALK ABOUT OTHER WOMEN. Eventually you'll want to both share stories and meanings from past romances, but for a relationship just getting off the ground it's probably too much of a strain. So save that kind of stuff.

More important, don't talk about other women you might now be seeing or even just find yourself attracted to. The demon Jealousy, lurking in even the sweetest of creatures, can be summoned with merely a bold glance at another woman while you're crossing the street together. One of your highest priorities should be to keep jealousy out of your relationships. It is definite poison. If you do find yourself attracted to, or even casually involved with, another woman, there is no need to make it an issue. If it doesn't just blow over, it will become an issue soon enough anyway.

SERVE HER BREAKFAST IN BED. This is probably the greatest social innovation since the massage and will always be *greatly* appreciated.

TAKE CARE OF HER WHEN SHE'S SICK. There is no better way to ingratiate yourself to someone and to do her an immense amount of good at the same time. What does this entail? No, you don't need to be constantly by her bedside. But by bringing her a meal, aspirin, or some books to read or by taking the time to play a game of checkers with her, you can transform this period into a relatively pleasant one for her.

TAKE HER TO YOUR GRANDMOTHER'S HOUSE FOR DINNER. Your grandmother is probably two things—the best cook you know and, more important, your biggest fan. At what restaurant could you not only get a great meal for free, but have the cook/waitress/third guest talk about nothing else than what a beautiful child you were, how well you always did in school, and why your girlfriend is lucky to be going out with you. Sure, it may get to be a little heavy-handed, but it really can't hurt for your girlfriend to hear those kinds of things.

The other reason to bring your girlfriend to your grandmother's house (if you don't have a grandmother, make it your favorite aunt) is to gradually introduce her to your family and your past. This will give her a deeper—and probably more affectionate—sense of who you are.

MAKE LOVE TO HER REGULARLY. Strange as it may sound, a lot of guys lose interest in sex with a woman once they actually get involved with her. This is because the novelty wears off and sex turns out to be not quite so purely blissful an experience as they had imagined. It takes work, patience, energy, and determination, since making love correctly to a woman you care about involves a good deal more than reaching orgasm. Her needs have to be considered just as much as your own.

Nevertheless, making love should not be feared or abandoned. It should be worked at and improved upon. Because simply put, there is no substitute. It is, and will always be, the most profound way of saying *"I Love you."*

KEEP ON MAKING HER FEEL SPECIAL. What this takes, above anything else, is continuing to *think* of her as special. Don't let her become a mundane, ordinary part of your life. A woman resents nothing more than that and ultimately will find someone else if neglected or subordinated in importance long enough.

If she does indeed lose her importance to you, ask yourself why. Are you simply being spoiled and indulgent, or have you naturally grown apart because of fundamental personality differences? If it's the latter, you should be as open and honest with her as you can. These dialogues need not necessarily be painful. People can split up without resentment or a sense of loss. It all depends how it's handled.

If it's the former, however, get off your ass and start treating her right. This includes everything I've suggested here, plus whatever else you can think of. Flowers, taking her out, other small gifts, etc. Put energy into it. Remember: Winning with women is an ongoing process, one that will continue the rest of your life, whether you date a hundred or settle down with one for keeps.